D0278772

Life of a Teenager in Wartime London

Life of a Teenager in Wartime London

Duncan Leatherdale

PEN & SWORD HISTORY

First published in Great Britain in 2017 by
Pen & Sword History
An imprint of
Pen & Sword Books Ltd
47 Church Street
Barnsley
South Yorkshire
S70 2AS

Copyright © Duncan Leatherdale, 2017

ISBN 978 1 47389 496 9

A CIP catalogue record for this book is
available from the British Library.

Printed and bound in England
By TJ International, Padstow, Cornwall PL28 8RW

Pen & Sword Books Ltd incorporates the Imprints of Pen & Sword Books
Archaeology, Atlas, Aviation, Battleground, Discovery, Family History, History,
Maritime, Military, Naval, Politics, Railways, Select, Transport, True Crime,
Fiction, Frontline Books, Leo Cooper, Praetorian Press, Seaforth Publishing,
Wharncliffe and White Owl.

For a complete list of Pen & Sword titles please contact
PEN & SWORD BOOKS LIMITED
47 Church Street, Barnsley, South Yorkshire, S70 2AS, England
E-mail: enquiries@pen-and-sword.co.uk
Website: www.pen-and-sword.co.uk

Contents

Foreword

I was fifteen-and-a-half-years old, living with my parents and brother in Dulwich in southeast London when the Second World War started. It was school holiday time and I was staying with friends in their house in Cornwall having, as it turned out, a last idyllic peacetime holiday. Midway during the holiday the terrible realisation that war was actually going to happen became obvious so I caught a train back to London.

I shall always remember the atmosphere of apprehension as, at each stop, more and more uniformed men boarded the train. Then I was standing in our living room, by the radio, as Neville Chamberlain stated that we were now at war.

My mother burst into tears. One has to remember hers was the generation that only twenty-one years before had been overjoyed at the Armistice following the First World War. My father had fought on the Western Front from 1914 to 1917 before being discharged, having had a hand shattered by shrapnel. Now, with two teenage children, it was all happening again – the pain, suffering and worry. Of course, I had no idea of the pain that generation, with memories so fresh, would be going through. In fact, it wasn't until I had my own children that I understood.

The following Sunday morning the sirens sounded. My father had reinforced the cellar of our old Edwardian house in the manner of the trenches in the earlier war – great, solid pillars of wood supporting the walls and ceiling. We went down there, I can clearly remember my knees shaking uncontrollably due to my fear. I'm glad to say I don't believe this ever happened again. Anyway, it was only a false alarm. For a period this absence of the expected air raids continued.

Initially my parents suggested I should go live with relatives in New Zealand for the duration of the war. I thought this was a very bad idea. I even opted out of evacuating to Brighton with my school, so the summer of 1939 saw the end of my schooling. What to do with me then? My brother, being four years older, had already applied for service in the RAF, so he was taken care of. It was decided I should attend Pitman's College for a course in shorthand and typing.

When I turned seventeen, I made a career change. I was given a job in Barclays Bank in City Road. This was rather fun. I was the first female to ever darken the walls of 146 City Road, therefore the staff did not quite know how to deal with me. I was, of course, the lowest of the low in terms of office hierarchy, but I was female, and as such I was treated with great respect. By that time, the daylight raids over London had begun. Often, as the sirens sounded, we would descend to the strong room below the bank for shelter.

I would travel daily by bus from my home to the Oval underground station, from where I completed the journey by tube. Invariably there were many people still lying on the platforms after having sought sanctuary there from the nighttime air raids. We had to step over them to get to the carriages. One particular day, after a big incendiary-bomb raid during the night, there were no buses running from my house to the Oval, so I set out to walk. I vividly remember stepping over the great hoses that bisected the road through Brixton, and the acrid smell of the burning that was still going on. Once at the tube station, all was well. I was a little late for work that day but the reason given was accepted by my manager.

My next career change took place when I turned eighteen. I started on a three-year course to become a physiotherapist at Guy's Hospital, situated on the south bank next to London Bridge. Again, this meant travelling from my home in Dulwich each day. At that time, I found working in one of the great London hospitals inspiring and spiritually strengthening. I felt it a privilege to be part of it and made friends for life there.

Certain incidents I remember of this period involved rockets and flying bombs. On one train journey to the hospital, a rocket landed a little ahead of us beside the track. The train was perched precariously on the bank, so we were not allowed to vacate it. Houses had been hit. The heart-rending vision of people being rescued from the debris, some alive, others dead, stayed with me forever. Eventually we were allowed to leave the train, walking the remainder of the journey to London Bridge along the track.

We students also worked for a while at a unit of Guy's at Orpington in southeast London, where badly injured service personnel were sent. One day, as I left West Dulwich station, a flying bomb passed in the opposite direction. I heard the engine stop, prior to it falling and exploding. I knew it was heading for the home I had just left. I phoned home as soon as I arrived at Orpington. To my relief, I found our house had been missed. Sadly, however, the bomb had fallen and demolished the house of good friends. The mother of the family was killed. The rest of the family, however, had not been in the house at the time. They came to live with us until they could be housed elsewhere.

It may seem surprising, but there were many happy memories as well. My New Zealand cousins had given their various boyfriends our London address, which they made their base during the war. They were all in the navy and left all their gear at our house when they went off on operations. We never knew when they would return, but there was always the fun when they returned on a spot of leave. The house would ring with merriment as we danced and sang around the piano. For today's youth, this may seem boring in the extreme. To us in those times, however, it was all we could wish for – these young men were back again and unharmed, at least for the moment.

We spent many nights down in our cellar. During one raid, our house was straddled by a stick of bombs. Two very nearly hit us, but luckily, for us at least, they landed in gardens on either side of our house. The shaking and vibration was, I imagined, as an earthquake would have felt. There were a number of us sleeping in the cellar that night, including one of our New Zealand friends. The whole house juddered. We were covered in layers of plaster from the cellar roof, while our naval friend slept peacefully through it all. We teased him about it afterwards. We concluded, however, that his life on the ocean wave in wartime – being depth-charged and bombed at sea – had rendered him immune to a mere air raid on land.

I also spent much of my time studying down in the cellar during night-time raids. When the subject was anatomy, I would have a skeleton with me – the real thing in those days, not the plastic jobs I believe they use now. I remember my father once commenting, 'It's bad enough having that racket going on above without seeing you surrounded by human bones.' He said it with a smile, being really quite pleased that I was taking my work seriously.

I remember a charm bracelet I had to have with me on these occasions. If the raid started and I had left it upstairs, I had to go and get it before I could concentrate again. I used to pin it to my underclothes when I took exams. It was a powerful source of comfort and support. I survived the war and passed my exams, so perhaps it worked. I still have the bracelet, although I don't wear it anymore.

For the first six months of 1943 I kept a diary. I wasn't much good at keeping it going though, so I stopped after June that year. I think I just got a bit bored of writing in it every day. When I read it now I can't help but think how foolish I sounded, worrying about my hair or some chap or other, but I suppose they were important to me at the time. Like so many people during that troubled period of our history, I wasn't going to let the small matter of the war stop me from living my life.

Glennis 'Bunty' Leatherdale, 2017.

Introduction

I t was a warm, summer's day, and I was sitting on the floral-patterned sofa in my grandmother's small living room when I first learned of her diary. She said she had found something of interest and, after rummaging in her large, dark-wood bureau, she produced a small, green leather book. I had a careful but cursory look through this little book, barely bigger than the palm of my hand, but quickly set it aside. The handwriting inside, some of it in pencil, some in ink, was too tricky to decipher during a quick read.

During this quick flick through, I noticed that the pencilled pages in particular were difficult to make out. So I offered to type them up so that Bunty could reread the words she had written some seventy years ago. I like to think that this was out of some desire to offer assistance and pleasure to her. Alternatively, perhaps it was some intuitive knowledge that, written on those small yellow pages, were fascinating glimpses into a forgotten but significant time. In truth though, I had recently bought a new laptop and just wanted something to do on it to justify the expense.

So, over a period of several weeks, I read through her diary, typing up each entry as I went. Some words I merely typed as question marks as I could not quite make them out. Others I guessed at, quite successfully as a later check with their original writer proved. As I worked my way through it, something surprising started to happen – I gradually became engrossed in the life of this teenage girl living in London during the Second World War. What had started as being simply a grandson's duty became the most interesting part of my day, a time when I could sit and read the inner thoughts of a young woman (an unfathomable mystery to me during the bulk of my life), and be exposed to a totally different time.

During those six months of 1943 in which she kept the diary, Bunty wrote accounts of air raids and the loss of friends, together with an analysis of Britain's military actions, and reports of patients she was treating in her role as a trainee physiotherapist at Guy's Hospital in central London. Much more interesting than all that, however, were the complaints familiar to teenagers throughout the ages – not being happy with one's appearance, the frustrations of the opposite sex, and the drudgery of exams and learning. It struck me how, even in a time of war, her biggest concerns were of the need to lose a bit of weight and how best to have her hair.

As I read, my interest became more than just that of a grandson reading his grandmother's memories. I wanted to know more about the world in which she was living. In fact, I rather forgot that the girl whose life I was glimpsing into was any relation of mine. I consequently thought that maybe these memories might have wider appeal. This was a firsthand account of life in war from a person belonging to a group whose voice is not often heard. There are numerous books about life on the home front, several of which I have read from cover to cover. These I have used to fill in the gaps of this world in which Bunty's diary was written. I found little reference, however, to life on the home front from a teenager's point of view. The point I found most interesting was that even though there was a war on, the normal angst of being a teenager was still ever-present.

To best understand Bunty's diary, one needs context, and that is what *Bunty's War* is all about. It is essentially a book of two parts. The first is to provide the context in which to read the second, thereby leaving Bunty's diary itself unaltered and unedited as much as possible. I wanted to try to understand what life was like generally for young people living in London during the Second World War.

In his book *The People's War*, Angus Calder said it was impossible to break up the home front into topics. To do so, he said, would be 'bound to falsify social history'. Naturally, I ignored his advice. I have based each chapter on separate topics that most interested me. This is not to say I disagree with him. Clearly, he is a great authority on the subject, and I would fully recommend giving *The People's War* a read if you want a more comprehensive history. However, for the sake of clarity in my own mind, I found it best to approach Bunty's War as a series of essays, each focusing on one particular issue.

Bunty's diary had raised several intriguing topic ideas in my mind, such as what entertainment was on offer during the black-out evenings? What holidays could a young person take? From a practical point of view, how did one commute around a war-torn city? Then there was the war itself. What was it like to live through an air raid? What did society expect of young people, how did one keep abreast of what was going on both on the home front and in foreign fields? Finally, what did they eat, and how did they make themselves look good? This is an issue familiar to teenagers of all generations. With such questions considered, hopefully the reader can then turn to Bunty's diary itself – all 157 entries made between Friday, 1 January and Thursday, 10 June 1943. This was the only diary she kept during the war. The fact that she managed to keep it going relatively unbroken (she only missed five entries) was surprising even to her. 'I just got bored keeping it,' she replied, simply, after I asked her why she did not write down more.

In some way it is frustrating that she kept the diary when she did. The first six months of 1943 were relatively dull from a war point of view. The Blitz was long gone and there were only intermittent raids on the city of London. However, though the raids may have been sporadic, they were no less deadly, as tragically demonstrated by the bombing of Sandford Road School in Catford. The war, however, was also far from being over. It would in fact be another two years before fighting ceased in Europe. The after effects were felt long afterwards, not least for those who had lost loved ones or had been injured. It was also because wartime measures, like rationing, did not suddenly stop just because the war had. Rationing actually remained in place until 4 July 1954, when restrictions were finally lifted on bacon and meat.

Bunty's war began as everyone's did with an announcement on the wireless from Prime Minister Neville Chamberlain. He was the very man who, just twelve months before, had waved a piece of paper to the press that he claimed would avoid any global conflict. This was only twenty years after the end of the worst war in history, a ground-breaking event that claimed the lives of some seventeen-million people. As a result, Britain's desire to keep the peace with an ever-expanding Germany, led by Adolf Hitler and his National Socialist party, was perhaps understandable.

Sadly, Hitler's desire for a German empire under the Third Reich did not end with the annexation of parts of Czechoslovakia, which Britain had accepted under the Munich Agreement signed in the early hours of 30 September 1938. After Hitler's Nazi army invaded Poland, Britain and her allies were left with little choice but to come to that country's defence – the Second World War had arrived barely two decades after the first had ended.

Bunty was just fifteen-and-a-half-years old when, at quarter past eleven on the morning of Sunday, 3 September 1939, she and her family gathered around the wireless to hear Mr Chamberlain make the following announcement on the BBC:

> This morning, the British Ambassador in Berlin handed the German government a final note stating that, unless we heard from them by eleven o'clock that they were prepared at once to withdraw their troops from Poland, a state of war would exist between us.

I have to tell you now that no such undertaking has been received,
and that consequently, this country is at war with Germany.

Bunty had ended a holiday in Cornwall early so that she could get home
before war was declared. She has often said that the scenes of young people
enjoying one last summer before war in Rosamund Pilcher's *Coming Home*,
reminded her of that holiday. The growing fears of another global conflict
clouded the joys of youthful summer. An air-raid siren sounded soon after
Chamberlain's speech and many feared this was it – the Germans had
arrived. It was just a false alarm though, and one of many during the first
few months of the war. It was a time of heightened tension, but a lack of
action on the home front resulted in it being dubbed the 'Bore War' or the
'Phony War'. Some even spoke of their frustration at the lack of activity. If
they were indeed at war they wanted to get on with it. Eventually they got
their wish as, on 7 September 1940, the Blitz began.

Bunty spent the whole war living in London with her parents Alfred
and Gertrude, and brother Peter (before he joined the RAF) in a large
town house in Dulwich. Her fuller story can be found scattered throughout
Bunty's War, specifically in the chapter before her actual diary entries, so I
won't dwell on it here, except to say she had absolutely no desire to join her
schoolmates in being evacuated.

I have received dozens of cards and letters from Bunty over the years,
from wishing me a happy birthday to showing me an amusing photograph she
took of a pigeon nesting atop a traffic light. Each one is written in her unique
squiggly style, often with a thick pen, and sometimes requiring a bit of time
and thought to decipher. It is odd then to see that very same handwriting
describing experiences familiar to me only from movies, documentaries
and books. I do not believe anyone ever thinks of their grandparents as
being anything but their grandparents. Bunty is my gran, and as far as I
am concerned, that is all she has ever been. So reading her diary has been
a pertinent prick to that arrogance of self-centredness, a poignant story of
another generation's toils and troubles in times of war. Thankfully, hers is an
experience I have not had to go through, due in no small part to the fact that
so many people were compelled to go through it between 1939 and 1945.

Of course, Bunty's war was not just Bunty's war. Her experiences were
shared by millions.

So when building the world in which her diary was written, I looked for
other firsthand accounts, specifically of teenagers and young people, and
of life at that time, particularly in London. The *Mass Observation* report

was useful, I refer to several entries made by two diarists in particular. The British Library proved most helpful in accessing the *Mass Observation* report archives. The *Mass Observation* was formed in 1937 by a group of people who wanted to record the actual thoughts and feelings of the British public on a huge range of issues. These opinions were gathered by survey and by people volunteering to keep diaries documenting their daily lives. These were then filed in the project's archives. Should you find yourself near the British Library with an hour or two to kill, I recommend having a browse.

I also turned to the Imperial War Museum and the diaries of three people in particular. Teenager Geoffrey Dellar kept a very comprehensive log of the air raids he lived through. Though lacking in emotional input – the entries being more about capturing facts than feelings – his ten notebooks proved a valuable resource. In particular, his description of life on the ground during a raid offered a great insight, while his cataloguing of a journey through London after a raid made for a fascinating read. The papers of Joyce Weiner were also exceedingly helpful, containing much of the emotion that Dellar had withheld from his writings. Joyce was much more poetic in her descriptions of raids, offering a different perspective. It was the third diary I found stored at the Imperial War Museum, however, that proved the most invaluable – the papers of John L. Sweetland.

Sweetland was 12 when war began and 17 when it ended. He was an only child, living with his parents in a large block of flats near Camden Town. In 1945, he wrote a forty-eight-page memoir based on diaries and contemporaneous notes he had kept through the war. It was to this manuscript that I turned. He talks of being evacuated, returning to London, the difficulty of finding a school, the drama of air raids, and the mix of exhilaration and exhaustion from night after night of bombs being dropped. During the war, he graduated from college, where he had to lie about his age to be accepted in the first place. He got a job in the civil service, and then had to sit and wait for the call-up. He talks of playing games with his friends, going for bike rides through bomb-damaged streets, finding a girlfriend, and coming face to face with fatalities of the Blitz. His memoirs are to the whole war what Bunty's diary is to the first six months of 1943. It is a window into the world and mind of teenagers living in London at the time.

All reasonable efforts were made to contact the three diary keepers through the Imperial War Museum. The details for the copyright holders of Sweetland and Joyce Weiner's diaries were no longer held by the museum. They suggested I publish them with a disclaimer making clear efforts have been made to source copyright holders. I am very grateful for their advice.

They did, however, send my request to use parts of Dellar's diary to his family, but sadly my letter was returned unopened, suggesting that their details are now out of date. Again, the museum suggested that I use his memories. Every individual, in their own way, gives an idea of what life was like in London during the Second World War. I hope by the end of *Bunty's War* that you too will have some idea of a young Londoner's lot between 1939 and 1945.

Finally, living as I do in northern England, I am fully aware that the Luftwaffe's attacks affected far more than simply London. Though this book is focused on the capital city, as that is where Bunty was living, I prefer to think of it as a tribute to all those people and places attacked during the Second World War.

Chapter One

London Life

In the summer of 1939, London was the largest city in the world. With more than 8.6 million residents, the capital city was home to almost twenty per cent of the nation's citizens. It was not until January 2015 that London could once again be called home by so many.

With world-famous parks, museums, hotels, shops, theatres and palaces, it was an exciting place to live. It was, however, also to become one of the main targets for the Luftwaffe's bombing raids, along with industrial hubs such as Liverpool, Coventry and Plymouth. The first German air-raiders came in July 1940, aiming for industrial and military targets. Two months later the most intense period of bombing began. The Blitz, as it became known, was the term also used to describe air raids across Britain and Europe. London was not the only place to be blitzed.

Initially, the bombing of London was a mistake. Hitler had ordered that bombing be kept to industrial and military targets, but on 24 August 1940, so the story goes, Luftwaffe pilots got lost and mistakenly dropped their deadly loads on central London, igniting huge fires in the East End. The RAF retaliated by attacking Berlin directly, an offensive which Hitler had assured the German people would not be allowed to happen. In response, the Germans changed tack. The citizens and streets of London and her sister cities became the targets, as much as factories, military posts and airfields had already been.

On Saturday, 7 September 1940, the Blitz began in earnest. It had, according to Angus Calder in *The People's War: Britain 1939–1945*, been a 'splendid, beautiful summer day' spent by many sipping tea in their gardens. At about five o'clock in the afternoon, several hundred German bombers arrived to set fire to London's docks. Wave upon wave of bombers kept coming over the next eleven-and-a-half hours, setting the East End alight. This was the first Battle of London, a fight between civilians and incendiary devices.

'Where the bombs fell heroes would spring up by accident', wrote Angus Calder of the men and women who leaped into action to extinguish incendiary bombs before they erupted into far more ferocious and fatal fires.

Some 431 people were killed, a further 1,600 injured, and countless more left homeless on that first night.

During the night, the code word 'Cromwell' was issued to the Home Guard around the country, who knew then that they had to be prepared for an imminent invasion. Some even mistakenly rang the bells at their village churches, believing that the invasion was actually happening. Ringing of the bells was only supposed to occur once German paratroopers were actually seen in the air, descending on their targets.

The Germans lost forty-one aircraft that night, which was a significant number for a Luftwaffe that had been depleted by losses in the Battle of Britain air combat three months earlier. The British saw forty-four of their fighters planes destroyed and seventeen pilots killed during the first night of the Blitz. But their valiant efforts to repel the raiders over the following nights and days, during which many were forced to drop their bombs well before they reached the target areas, caused Hitler to postpone his imminent invasion plans.

Between 7 September 1940 and 21 May 1941, some 20,000 tons of high-explosive bombs were dropped on London, as well as on sixteen other British towns and cities. London was attacked seventy-one times, including on fifty-seven consecutive nights. About one million buildings were destroyed and 20,000 people, the vast majority civilians, killed.

Life on the ground, however, continued as Bunty's diaries attest, although there were some big changes the hardy Londoners had to get used to. For a start, there was the blackout that applied to everyone everywhere in the country. Knowing that war was coming, the government announced nationwide, compulsory blackout measures starting on 1 September 1939, two days before Neville Chamberlain's declaration-of-war speech.

During the hours of darkness, it was illegal to show a light lest you reveal a target for the aerial raiders. Blackout was stringently enforced, with fines for those who failed to adhere to it. Even just showing a chink of light could lead to a visit from the ARP wardens or police. Cries of 'put out that light!' echoed around the darkened streets. The start and finishing times for each night's blackout were published in the newspapers, so the courts offered little leniency to those who claimed ignorance, with jail terms of up to three months and fines of £100 at their disposal. Even lighting a cigarette outside was forbidden. In 1940, there were some 300,000 people charged with blackout offences across the country.

The government issued plenty of advice to householders on adhering to the blackout. One Board of Trade pamphlet, released under the 'Make Do and Mend' campaign, offered the following notes on how to best look after blackout curtains:

> Never wash blackout material – washing makes it more apt to let the light through. Instead, go over your curtains regularly with a vacuum cleaner if you have one; if not take them down at least twice a year, shake gently and brush well. Then iron them thoroughly – this makes them more light proof and also kills any moth eggs or grubs which may be in them.

The blackout was something of a health and safety nightmare. Incidents included tripping over steps, walking into sandbags, falling into canals, stepping off a train platform, and, as Angus Calder describes it, 'cannonading off a fat pedestrian'. American journalist Quentin Reynolds, in *The Wounded Don't Cry*, wrote:

> London is a ghost town at night. You never meet anyone on the street. Now and then the fire engines or ambulances would roar by you never see them as they carry only the smallest sidelights. The street crossings bother you at night. You never know when you've reached the kerb. Then you constantly bump into lamp-posts or pillar-boxes. Walking round London at night hardly comes under the head of good clean fun.

The first incident of a person dying on the home front as a direct consequence of the war, occurred on the first night of the blackout. A police officer, who had climbed up a drainpipe to reach an illegally illuminated window to chasten the guilty party, fell three storeys to his death. By December 1939, there were an average of forty fatal accidents a day, involving pedestrians and vehicles, an eight-fold increase on pre-war numbers. It is impossible to say these were all due to the blackout, but there was little doubt that having people and vehicles mixing in the dark could only lead to bad results for the people. Eight soldiers were severely injured on 31 October when a lorry drove into the back of them as they were marching during the blackout.

Some started to question the worth of the blackout when it was leading to so many casualties. One letter writer to *The Times* in November 1939 said:

> The chief reason for the present drastic restrictions on vehicular and street lighting is, I presume, to prevent loss of human life in

air-raids; but it may be gravely doubted if the deaths by such means would, in two months, have resulted in this holocaust caused by the blackout.

Many though, appreciated the need for total darkness, and although the Air Raid Precaution (ARP) wardens, who enforced the blackout, were perhaps unpopular, they were seen as a necessary annoyance. Another correspondent to *The Times* even offered the wardens the use of his rooftop garden so offenders showing lights at high-up windows, which were difficult to see from the street, could be detected and disciplined.

Kerbs and other street furniture were painted white to offer some orientation at night, while pedestrians were encouraged to wear white bands or buttons, or carry newspapers to mark them out to drivers. Posters were put up advising motorists how to best prepare their vehicles. Headlights on cars and vehicles had to be masked so that only a small crescent of light was beamed on to the road, while side lamps and rear lights were to be dimmed. Only one eighth of an inch of indicator was allowed to be seen, and all dashboard lights had to be covered. This made it quite tricky for nighttime drivers to know if they were keeping to the newly imposed 20 mph speed limit.

Drivers tended to stick closely to the white line down the middle of the road, which caused more than a few head-on collisions. The *Autocar* magazine, which was launched in 1895 and is still being published weekly, even mooted going French and driving on the right so motorists could follow the white–painted kerb, but their suggestion never gained momentum.

Drivers also had to paint parts of their cars white, such as the bumpers, running boards and mudguards. They could be prosecuted if the painted areas became dirty. It was also illegal to park facing oncoming traffic. Some also hung large pieces of cards at each end to try and make their vehicle more conspicuous to other street users.

Car accidents soared as a result of the lack of light. Within a few months, it was estimated that about one in five people had suffered some sort of injury as a result of the blackout, be it being struck by a car or tripping over an unseen obstacle. While it was a dangerous time to be out, some relished the blackout for the cover it provided for nefarious doings. The number of assaults carried out under the protection of darkness rose. The streets were not always a safe place to be, especially for young women who may find themselves the victims of unwanted and sometimes forceful attention.

After a few months, the government did relax the rules slightly in a bid to curb the number of injuries. For example, people were allowed to carry torches as long as the beam was damped with tissue paper. When the air-raid siren sounded, however, this action was again banned. The frustrating truth was, however, that even with the city's lights blacked out, German bombers could still find their way around London on bright nights thanks to the River Thames that wound its way through it. Quentin Reynolds in *The Wounded Don't Cry* wrote:

> We curse bright nights when the moon is full. On a night like this, the Thames would be a white ribbon of milk pointing towards London. You can't blackout the Thames, and the Thames tells the German bombers everything they want to know about London.

The blackout finally ended on 17 September 1944, when the threat of aerial raids had seemingly diminished. London was still attacked, however, but no longer by the manned bombers of the Blitz. A new threat arrived – the pilotless V-1 launched from mainland Europe towards Great Britain. When the engine stopped, the flying bomb dropped, causing huge destruction wherever it fell. The general rule was that as long as you could hear it, you were safe, but once it fell silent, you knew it was coming down. This was the danger of the 'Doodlebug', the nickname given these rockets.

The first V-1 fell in east London early in the morning of 13 June. It was reported that the explosive power of a V-1 was the equivalent of a one-ton bomb, and that whole streets could be obliterated by just one missile. London was the target of a German regime in the last throes of war. It is estimated that ninety-two per cent of V-1 casualties were in the capital. The threat was decreasing by September, as Allied forces seized the European launch sites, but a new menace was looming – the V-2. The V-2 was bigger and more powerful than its older brother, but its attacks were more sporadic. When it found its target, the V-2 was monstrous. Londoner Myrtle Solomon, in *Forgotten Voices of the Second World War* wrote:

> The Doodlebugs were pretty frightening but the V-2s were terrifying. Perhaps we were tired by that point in the war but we were much more scared than when the bombs were raining down on us during the Blitz. I was longing for the end by then.

About 160 people were killed and many more buried in rubble when one hit a shop in South East London in November. Initially, to avoid causing public panic or letting the enemy know their unmanned bombs were finding their targets, the government refused to admit that the missiles existed. The damage they caused was instead attributed to domestic failures such as explosions of gas mains. Again, as the Germans were being vanquished, the number of rockets being fired at London declined, and eventually disappeared. Throughout the bombings by both the Luftwaffe and the V rockets, the people of London still went out to restaurants, cinemas, bars and theatres.

One threat that thankfully failed to materialise was the dreaded gas attacks. The First World War had shown the horrors that toxic gas could cause. In the months leading up to the Second World War, it was feared that such chemical weaponry would be used against Britain's civilians. In the months leading up to the anticipated, and feared unavoidable war, the government issued gas masks to every man, woman and child in the country, some thirty-eight million in total. People were urged, as best possible, to make their homes airtight against gas. Cracks and keyholes needed filling, and were often pasted over with newspaper, while doorframes were smothered in blankets. Yellow gas-detection paint was applied to the top of post boxes, which would change colour in the event of a gas attack. People could be fined if they were found out of the house without a gas mask on them.

Naturally, the more fashion conscious found a way to carry their masks in large bags, thereby maintaining their stylish looks. Some fashion firms even released special ranges of gas-mask carriers that came with matching handbags and purses. Just as with their enforcement of the blackout, however, the ARP wardens who made sure people were carrying their gas masks irked readers of *The Times*.

The Home Office issued guidelines saying people should have their gas masks with them if they were going at least seven minutes away from their home or workplace. One Ronald Woodham wrote to the paper and said:

> I live less than two minutes' distance from my place of work, I am expected by the local wardens to carry my mask at all times. Here is yet another instance of that excess of zeal on the part of the local ARP workers which is rapidly making the nation a laughing-stock.

The wardens were responsible, however, for alerting civilians to a gas attack through the use of a large wooden rattle. As it turned out, gas was not one of Hitler's chosen weapons, but the government wanted the people to be prepared.

Preparations also included offering people places of shelter from the anticipated avalanche of bombs expected to fall on their heads. Many, like

Bunty's father, chose to fortify their basements and cellars as a haven for when the bombs fell. Others built Anderson shelters in their back gardens – small, self-assembly, metal shelters partly dug into the earth. These were issued free to households that earned £250 or less a year, but it cost £7 to those who earned more. The shelter comprised of plates of galvanised steel erected over a pit dug into the earth. They offered protection from flying debris but could do little in the event of a direct hit.

In 1941, the Morrison shelter came into circulation. It was essentially a large steel cage that could be built inside the home. This meant that people could at least stay in the relative warm during air raids. Its solid top meant the shelter was often used as a table. The Morrison shelter was designed to withstand the weight of an upper floor of a house falling on it and, like the Anderson, was a self-assembly job. It was free to households who earned less than £350 a year.

Some chose not have a shelter at all. Jonathan Sweetland, a youngster living with his parents in Camden, said neither his mother nor his father wanted one. He wrote in his memoirs, held by the Imperial War Museum, that they would instead spend nights trying in vain to sleep beneath the dining room table, the noise of bombs falling, buildings being struck, guns and planes making sleep all but impossible. He wrote:

> We just lay there with the cacophony of the planes, bombs and guns about us, feeling the building sway when a bomb fell close and watching the chandelier become more of a pendulum as it swung back and forth with the building.

They were fully clothed and ready to flee at a moment's notice. In a small tin box held by his mother, were kept the most valuable family papers as well as some cash.

Many other Londoners went to public shelters while large numbers used the underground, which first opened in 1863 to allow people to travel around the city without getting their heads wet. The government was initially reluctant to let people seek shelter in the underground network for health and safety reasons. There were fears about hygiene. The inadequacy of the toilets were given as just one example of why having so many people staying in the underground stations would pose a problem. The authorities had also earmarked the underground tunnels as storage space for the hundreds of thousands of bodies they feared would result from the German air raids. The public persisted, however, and in September 1940, the government took active steps to make the underground an official shelter. 'They were dry, warm, well-lit and the raids were inaudible', wrote Angus Calder in *The People's War.*

Some fifteen miles of platforms and tracks at seventy-nine stations were used as shelters. The record occupancy for one night was 177,000 in September 1940, soon after the commencement of the Blitz. One stretch of uncompleted track, starting at Liverpool Street and running beneath the East End, became a refuge for 10,000 Londoners. As there was no need to get out of the way of trains, there are reports of some people spending several weeks at a time down there.

Most of the stations used as shelters were also still running train services, creating a situation where some were trying to sleep or simply hold onto their spot, while others were stepping around or over them trying to board the trains. In her diary, Bunty vividly recalls making her way between sleeping people on the platforms the morning after a raid as she travelled to work. Diplomat and author Harold Nicholson, who was married to poet Vita Sackville-West, recorded in his diary on 1 March 1944, his dislike of seeing people in such uncomfortable conditions:

> It is sad to see so many people sleeping on the tube platforms. It is more disgraceful than ever to see the Americans with the East End Jewish girls shouting among those unhappy and recumbent forms. I hate it.

To keep space clear for commuters from those seeking shelter, the platform was divided by two white lines. One was eight feet away from the track edge, and until 7.30 pm tube 'residents' had to stay behind it. The other was four feet closer to the platform's edge, creating an area between the two white lines that may be encroached upon and inhabited between 8 pm and 10.30 pm. After 10.30 pm, when the trains had stopped running for the day, the whole tube station became fair game. There were reports of people slinging up hammocks above the track and using the dark tunnel at either end of the station as toilets. In her memoirs, *Forgotten Voices of the Second World War*, Elizabeth Quayle said:

> When you came back at night on the underground, of the entire platform only a bit – the eighteen inches or maybe two foot – near the edge was left, and all the rest were rows of people with their belongings, cats and dogs and children. They were as good-tempered as it was possible to be.

Though people put on a brave and friendly face, comfortable they were not. Where humans gathered, so too did unwanted creatures such as lice and mosquitoes. The stations, at least, offered a sense of safety, being far below ground from the bombers.

'This is how thousands of families live at night in London – far under the ground', wrote American journalist Quentin Reynolds in *The Wounded Don't Cry*. One night he made his way through Camden Town tube station where he saw people playing cards and singing songs such as *The Nightingale Sang in Berkeley Square*, accompanied by a man playing his accordion. Reynolds adds:

> The Underground dwellers impose a nine o'clock curfew on themselves. The accordion player pillowed his head on the accordion, a heavy quiet settled over the reclining forms. The guns and the bombs seemed far away. A train pulled in. Those who were asleep never woke, for noise is so much a part of our existence in London these nights that it is only quiet that disturbs us because it seems unnatural. It may be cold down there and the air sticky with the feel of hundreds of people packed together, but it's safe.

The tube station, however, could not guarantee absolute safety and shelter. At Balham Station in 1940, sixty-eight people were killed when a bomb detonated directly overhead. The explosion tore through the road, causing rubble, sand and water to fall onto those on the platform below. A further 111 were killed at Bank in January 1941, when a high-explosive bomb caused the booking hall and circular gallery to collapse.

In *Wartime Britain 1939–1945*, Juliet Gardiner reported witnesses seeing people electrocuted after the blast threw them onto the live rail tracks. Another 178 died at Bethnal Green in 1943, when an explosion provoked mass panic. The sound drove hundreds to try to enter the station, causing a huge and fatal crush.

Inevitably, having so many people in one place also offered opportunities for criminals. The stations could get very crowded, providing conmen with an opportunity to devise a scheme in which they would charge people for sleeping spots, their lackeys holding places on the platforms until payment had been made. Some parts of the underground network were closed, such as the Holborn to Aldwych branch on the Piccadilly line, to store treasures and artefacts from the British Museum.

Numerous contemporary reports and historical accounts highlight the great defiance many people felt and showed during the war years. Yes, they were at war, and many had loved ones fighting on front lines in Europe, Africa and Asia. In Britain, there was a constant threat of aerial attacks or invasion, but people were determined to carry on living their lives just as they always had done. There are accounts of some families, like Sweetland's, refusing air-raid shelters, saying that if they were to die then let it be in their own beds. The spirit of Londoners during it all remained resolute. The famous Blitz spirit they showed has become synonymous with people banding together in the face of adversity.

Businesses tried to carry on as normally as possible. Pubs, shops and cafes, which had lost windows in the air raids, put up signs declaring themselves 'more open than usual'. The owner of one badly bombed bookshop remained defiant by putting up a notice saying the shop was 'very wide open' and had 'plenty of blasted books'. One pub sign read, 'Our windows are gone but our spirits are excellent.' In her diaries, Joan Strange, a young woman from Worthing, noted a sign put up by a news vendor that had caught her attention: 'Houses down, shops down, churches down but we are not down', he had written in chalk next to his sales spot.

'Good old Londoners', Joan wrote on 16 November 1940. She also saw for herself the condition of those seeking shelter in the underground stations: 'The sanitary arrangements are bad but the people are good natured and stick their concrete beds well.' On another visit, Joan was struck by how full of people London was, adding, 'It was difficult to realise a war was on except for the balloon barrage, presence of soldiers and the blackout.'

In a letter to *The Times*, a reader recounted the experience of an air-raid warden in southwest London during one particularly busy night in September 1940:

> After one particularly loud crash, a warden dashed out into the darkness and, skirting a crater in the road, came to a pile of bricks which had until recently been a house. Climbing over some of these he called, 'Is anybody there?'
>
> From the depths, a male voice replied, 'Yes, an old lady and myself.'
>
> 'Is she alright?' called the warden.
>
> 'No,' said the voice, 'she's a little bothered to know where she is going to spend the rest of the night.'

The warden, the correspondent noted, was called out nearly twenty times that night.

As always, British humour helped keep the spirits up.

'If Marshal Goering's young men go on bombing Buckingham Palace they will make it unfit for occupation by Herr Hitler during his triumphal visit to our shores', wrote one reader to *The Times*. 'Happily', they concluded, 'two previous invaders of England have left another royal residence, the Tower of London, where he could be housed as he deserves. His acceptance of a suite of apartments in the Bloody Tower would give widespread satisfaction.'

It is worth noting that Buckingham Palace remained the main home of King George VI and Queen Elizabeth throughout the war. The palace was hit nine times by bombs, the worst of which was in 1940 when the palace's chapel was demolished. Afterwards, Queen Elizabeth famously said: 'I am glad we have been bombed, now we can look the East End in the face.'

Doris Scott, who lived in Canning Town in east London, said the public also appreciated the palace being hit. 'If we knew that they had a hit it made us feel better because it brought them down to our level,' she said in *Forgotten Voices of the Second World War*. 'They did inspire people in their own way,' she added.

On another occasion in 1943, a plot of Brussels sprouts being grown in the palace gardens was all but destroyed by an air raid. Having the Royal family by their sides, going through the same experiences, was a real boost for the ordinary citizens of London. Many appreciated them staying in London when they could have retreated to the country. One man wrote, 'Our King and Queen are contending with war magnificently carrying on here in their capital when they could be miles away in safety, this is the King and Queen of whom we are so proud.'

There were other features in London, aside from bomb–damaged buildings and darkened neighbourhoods, which showed it was at war. A booklet issued to American servicemen being deployed to Britain warned:

Every light in England is blacked out every night and all night. Every highway signpost has come down and barrage balloons have gone up. Grazing land is now ploughed for wheat and flowerbeds turned into vegetable gardens. Britain's peacetime army of a couple of hundred thousand has been expanded to over two million men. Everything from the biggest factory to the smallest village workshop is turning out something for the war.

Up to forty barrage balloons were hoisted over London, which, according to writer Wilfrid Sheed, looked like 'ads for a coming circus'. They were some sixty-six feet long, thirty-feet high and filled with 20,000 cubic feet of hydrogen – all with the express purpose of deterring low-flying aircraft from swooping in over the city. Each was tethered to a lorry or the ground by a long, steel winch-operated cable manned by a crew. They even inspired several children's book characters, such as Blossom the Brave Balloon, Bulgy, and Boo-Boo the Barrage Balloon.

In 1939, with conflict looming, trenches were dug in the parks. The Home Office had issued an edict to councils in highly populated areas, instructing that enough trenches should be dug to provide protection for up to ten per cent of the population. The main purpose of these ditches scarring London's green and pleasant parks was to provide refuge for those caught out and about during an air raid.

The first of the trenches ran in straight lines for up to forty yards, but they were quickly identified as potential death traps in the event of an explosion. Subsequent trenches, emulating that of the Great War, were dug in zig-zag formations. By the end of September 1939, about one-million feet of trenches had been dug.

'Within a few weeks most had several inches of water in the bottom and were crumbling at the edges', notes Philip Ziegler in his 1995 work *London At War*. Unsurprisingly perhaps, they were not well-liked by the public. On the first night of the Blitz, more than 1,450 people crammed into the trenches that had been dug through Bethnal Green's Victoria Park. They spent most of the night standing shoulder to shoulder in about three inches of water. Church crypts were also transformed into public air-raid shelters. One such example was at St Martins-in-the-Fields, where thousands of coffins, containing the remains of the dead, were removed to enable the living to shelter there in an attempt to avoid them joining their ancestors. Public shelters were not for the faint-hearted, thanks mainly to woefully inadequate toilet facilities, but, where built correctly, they also saved many lives.

Some 29,890 Londoners were killed in air raids during the war according to T.H. O'Brien's 1955 work *History of the Second World War: Civil Defence*. For comparison, that is slightly more than a capacity crowd at Lord's Cricket Ground. A further 50,507 (an eighty-three per cent crowd at the Olympic Stadium) were admitted to hospital, most of them with serious injuries, while another 88,842 (about 1,500 short of filling Wembley Stadium) were slightly injured. The worst period was between 7 September and 31 December 1940, when 13,339 died and 17,937 seriously injured.

Another high-casualty year was 1944, with 7,533 killed and 19,661 hospitalised. According to figures from London County Council, by March

1945, the city's rescue service had attended 16,396 incidents, saved 22,228 injured, and seen 54 of its own personnel killed and 1,041 injured. Some 73,073 buildings were totally destroyed. A further 43,410 were damaged beyond repair, 161,643 seriously damaged but repairable, 126,281 damaged but habitable, and 1,399,241 slightly damaged, the District Surveyors Association reported.

Obviously all this damage meant there was a lot of debris to clear up. According to the District Surveyors Association, some 140 million bricks were salvaged, 340,000 tons of metal retrieved and 14 million tons of cartage collected.

On 5 July 1941, Joan Strange wrote, 'In Hyde Park there is a central dump for rubble, etc – it's a young mountain with a road over it. I wonder how many houses have helped make it – thousands?'

All of these records have been compiled by Laurence Ward in *The London County Council Bomb Damage Maps 1939–1945*. He said that just identifying which buildings were which was a challenge after an air raid, such was the mess and devastation wrought by the bombs.

The surveyors were 'faced with ruined, dangerous buildings, running the gauntlet of unexploded bombs and collapsing walls to create the best possible record of the damage'. By 19 June 1941, more than two-million houses across Britain had been damaged or destroyed, of which about sixty per cent were in London. By the end of the war, 3,750,000 had been hit – about two in seven – of which 250,000 were beyond repair. In central London, just one in every ten houses avoided any damage at all. Historian Jerry White, in his book *London in the Twentieth Century*, described the damage as 'desolation on a Pompeian scale'. He adds, 'Acres of housing had been laid waste in the East End and Dockside. Great rents in London's fabric scarred nearly every neighbourhood'.

As terrible as it was, the utter destruction of the East End slums did bring about some good.

Plans had already been underway to redevelop the area to get rid of the squalid and cramped streets. The Luftwaffe did half the job for the developers. Much of the subsequent replacement housing was a marked improvement on what had been there before. Stepney and Poplar, for example, were redesigned to house four people on a space where ten people had lived before the war.

By the end of May 1940, some 1,400,000 people, about one sixth of the city's population, had been homeless at some point because of the raids. In Stepney, four out of ten houses were damaged or destroyed. 'When you have been in the front line and taken it extra hard, the country wants to look after you', proclaimed a leaflet issued by the Ministry of Home Security in December, 1940, 'for you have suffered in the national interest as well as your own in the fight against Hitler. If your home is damaged there is a great deal of help ready for you.'

The leaflet directed people who had been left homeless, and had nowhere else to go, to rest centres where they could get food and temporary shelter while looking for somewhere else to live. These were meant to provide temporary accommodation for just a day or two, but some stayed several weeks in the centres, many of which were over-capacity, before moving on. Bomb victims could also get money, new ration books and identity cards, and a new gas mask, in addition to medical assistance for shock. The leaflet promised that those who could go and stay with relatives would be offered vouchers for free travel to get them there. Failing that, a new home would be found for them. There were also earnings–related grants available to replace essential furniture, clothes and tools.

If a home was repairable, the local authority would carry out the work if a landlord was unavailable. It could, however, take a while before they were able to do the job. Where a home was destroyed, compensation was available. Of course, some saw the opportunity to cheat the system, most famously perhaps Walter Handy, who falsely claimed to have been bombed out of his home nineteen times in five months. He was jailed for three years.

Many people left London of course, predominantly children who were moved to safer sites in the countryside, and young men of fighting age and women who joined the Land Girls Army. By 1944, London's population had dropped to about 5.45 million. Where evacuations occurred, it was not just people who made for safer climes, but some organisations also opted to leave London. The Bank of England, for example, took over Hurstbourne Park in Hampshire, while many of the patients of Great Ormond Street Children's Hospital were relocated to Tadworth Court, a site in Surrey the hospital had bought in 1927 and still uses today mainly for young people with brain injuries.

Bomb–damaged London was an exciting place for youngsters, offering new opportunities for exploration and discovery. Once bombing had started becoming much more infrequent, John Sweetland would enjoy cycling around London, enjoying the new vistas opened up by bomb damage and subsequent clearing. On some summer nights, he would take the tube to Aldersgate and then walk to Red Cross Street to admire the fire station 'standing symbolically untouched amidst the fire devastated area'. The firefighters themselves could often be found working their allotment across the road. The soil for the plots had been brought from Hampstead Heath, making the allotments home to various vegetables, as well as pigs and rabbits.

Throughout the war, Londoners, just as the British did in general, kept on going about their lives, trying to remain as ordinary as possible in their extraordinary circumstances. One 18-year-old civil servant summed up the mood and attitude of Londoners with a poem he wrote for the *Mass Observation* project in 1941. He composed the nine stanzas as he sat on a London and North Eastern Railway train bound for his home in northeast London. His poem tells the tale of four men sat around a fire, three of whom – a hunter, a sailor and a mountain climber – were bragging of their great bravery. The hunter had risked his life thousands of times taking on bears, lions and tigers while the sailor had survived storms and tempests in the middle of the sea. The mountain climber had scaled the world's highest peaks and braved death-defying drops. Finally, the fourth man, a small man wearing glasses and puffing on a pipe told his story. He had never sought danger nor coveted adventure and yet he was braver than them all, he proclaimed, for he had been a Londoner in 1941.

In his work *London in the Twentieth Century*, Jerry White wrote:

London never came close to the terminal dislocation that the Luftwaffe hoped for and the pre-war planners feared. It was so vast, its infrastructure so capable of finding ways round the damage, that it could absorb the blows and get on with life.

Chapter Two

Education and Evacuation

On 31 August 1939, with war now imminent and immediate air raids anticipated, the evacuations began. Whole schools were moved to safer places in the countryside, with children being placed with families and homeowners away from the cities. Nationally, about 1.5 million children and a further 400,000 teachers and school staff left the cities over four days. In London, some 376,652 school-age children and teachers were evacuated, along with 275,895 preschoolers and their mothers, 3,577 expectant mothers, and 3,403 blind adults. This does not take into account the estimated 800,000 or so who made their own way out of the city.

According to Angus Calder in *The People's War: Britain 1939–1945*, the sheer numbers took some of the reception centres by surprise. One group from Dagenham was taken away by boat to East Anglia. Due to a lack of organisation at the other end, mothers, children and teachers spent up to four days sleeping in school halls. There they had straw for mattresses and grain bags for blankets, while enjoying a diet of milk, apples and cheese.

It is fair to say that the evacuees' experiences were mixed. Some had a rollicking good time in the countryside, learning new things and enjoying a different sort of life away from the clutter and crowds of London's sometimes squalid streets. Others, however, had a disagreeable experience, not least those whose hosts treated them with apathy at best, and open hostility at worst.

John Sweetland's experiences fell mainly in the latter category. He and his classmates boarded a steam train at Marylebone Station bound for they knew not where. Eventually they alighted at a place called Brackley, a town in Northamptonshire some seventy miles north-west of London. After several hours wait – time they spent trying to catch frogs and throwing lumps of coal – the party was taken by coach to Buckingham where they were deposited at a town hall. They sat eating sandwiches and waiting while, two by two, they were called away to be sent off somewhere unknown.

In his memoirs Sweetland wrote, 'Evening wore on and I began to feel panicky. Supposing I was never called, the lights switched off and the grown-ups went home.' But eventually his name was called, and, together with an older boy he did not know, Sweetland was led out into a darkening town. He adds:

> The lack of organisation showed for it seemed that we must have walked every street in the town, stopping occasionally for our guide to knock on a door. This was repeated several times. The door would open, a few words would be exchanged, we would be inspected by torchlight and with a positive 'no', the door closed against us. To be fair, our appearance after the long day can't have been very appealing.

Eventually the pair were accepted, albeit reluctantly, by a single woman in her forties living with her elderly father in a large Victorian home opposite the town's cemetery. 'My stay at the house was not a happy one', Sweetland later wrote. He and the other boy shared a brass bed in the attic, having been told quite plainly by their hostess that they were not welcome. Once a week they had a bath in a Victorian cast-iron tub, which had to be carried up to them already filled with water. It was 'insufficient and cold' Sweetland noted. The food was not much better, although Sweetland did make a note of one highlight – he was allowed to lick the spoon his hostess had used to make a trifle for a dinner party with her friends.

Although many country folk were happy to take in evacuees, it is also true that some, like Sweetland's hostess, resented them. In his diary for the *Mass Observation* report, one student, after discussing their arrival in Reading with a friend, had his own views on evacuees. Many were dirty and they had written swear words on their hosts' bedroom walls, he noted with some disgust and annoyance. He also cited one or two as having ringworm. Two Italian boys, in particular, needed half-a-dozen baths to get all the dirt off of them. The older teenager felt that it was rather unfair on the people of Reading, especially parents who would now see their own children mixing with and picking up bad habits from the evacuees from the city slums. He did note that he did not blame the children or their parents. The situation was relatively unavoidable, but he did suggest that perhaps hostels should be used to house the evacuees rather than good people's good homes.

Although out of London, the evacuees still had to attend school. They were kept separate from the local children. Teaching was mainly in the form of listening to educational broadcasts on the BBC Home Service, interspersed with drill and games on the school playground and nature walks. Their weekend activities would hardly have helped endear the evacuees to their foster families. According to Sweetland, these were spent in 'rowdy pursuits around the High Street'. He writes:

> Most acquaintances of mine were unhappy with their lot and one or two were reported to have walked the fifty or so miles home to London which I contemplated doing myself while gazing at the wooden fingerpost which had not yet been removed, as a last resort. One exception was my pre-war friend who was billeted with the owners of a sweet shop, treated as one of the family and was the envy of many.

Within a few weeks of the mass evacuation, and with London still to be attacked, many children started to return to their city homes. Sweetland returned home five weeks after his evacuation, his hostess surprisingly unhappy at his leaving, writing: 'Since breaking the news, my Lady could hardly bring herself to speak to me and my departure was decidedly icy, doubtless due to the loss of the evacuees' lodging allowance.' The lodging allowance paid by the state consisted of ten shillings and sixpence for the first child, and then eight shillings and sixpence per additional child. Although happy to be heading home, Sweetland said he did enjoy his time as an evacuee:

> It's not an experience I would have missed. The beauty of the countryside and a night sky so full of brilliant stars had never been seen before. And it was an experience which I could embellish and relate to my friends left at home without fear of contradiction.

By January 1940, almost half of all London's evacuees had returned home, which posed a problem for the authorities – what to do about school? As Angus Calder notes, 'To reopen the schools would be to admit the failure of evacuation, but the Government could not hold back for long.' It was clear some schooling would be needed for those children still in London.

Writing in *Mass Observation* diaries in *We Are At War*, Londoner Eileen Potter, whose job it was to aid the evacuations, noted seeing some of the slummiest parts of the city being cluttered with 'dirty, neglected-looking children playing about aimlessly'. She said, 'The neglect of education may prove a greater danger to our civilisation than the falling of a few bombs.' Probably, like many children and young teenagers at the time, John Sweetland was not particularly disappointed at the lack of education on offer. 'Back home after five weeks of evacuation and filled with the elation of a perhaps never-ending holiday for schools were closed', he wrote, 'Maybe the war wouldn't be so bad.'

The authorities clearly agreed with the concerned Ms Potter rather than the excited John Sweetland. On 1 November 1939, schools in the evacuated area were permitted to reopen, apart from those in the most dangerous areas or ones without air-raid shelters. Two months later, about a quarter of the children in the evacuation areas were back in full-time education, while a similar number were attending school part-time, with another quarter or so being home-schooled.

When the air raids started proper however, schooling became trickier, although it did continue. 'School is a farce', noted Will, a teacher in Leytonstone, in a letter to his brother and sister-in-law published in Carol Harris' *Blitz Diary*: 'Only half or less of the boys attend and we spend our time in the corridors which are our shelter.' John Sweetland was thirteen at the time. He would have returned to his regular school, except its occupants, teachers and staff were still evacuees in Buckinghamshire. His father initially placed him in a small private school in Gloucester Avenue, which specialised in Latin and ancient Egyptian. Realising it was not really suitable for his son, he then found a college willing to take him in. The only problem was that they only took on pupils aged 16 or over.

Sweetland later wrote in his memoirs:

> At my preliminary interview the Head instructed me to lie about my age. I was to be sixteen and never to appear in short trousers. What embarrassment! Never mind the raids, there was I, thirteen years old and appearing in the streets amongst my friends in grown up's long trousers! The jeering! Who did I think I was?!

And so began Sweetland's education at the Technical Institute for the Distributive Trade on Charing Cross Road. Getting to know his new classmates, all of whom were at least three or four years older than him, and needed to believe he was their age, proved something of a steep learning curve. Sweetland wrote:

> I was certainly a puzzle to them and seemingly underdeveloped for a sixteen year old. One young man even inquired if I was a 'bum boy', but as I had no idea what was meant by this expression I was unable to answer. My solution to all this inquisitiveness was to keep a very low profile and keep out of trouble.

Of course, education was disrupted by air raids, so many 'classes' involved playing card games in the college's basement by candlelight. The call-up also derailed many an education. By October, there were only four students left in Sweetland's class, the rest having enlisted or been conscripted to join the forces. Eventually there was none, the college closed by a night-time bomb that fell through the gymnasium floor and exploded in the basement shelter. Had it been during the day, Sweetland and his classmates would surely have been killed. College did eventually restart, and in 1944, Sweetland, now aged 16, graduated. Finding work after finishing college, however, was a challenge. As the war was ongoing with no end date in sight, many employers knew that when they turned 18 their young male workers would probably be called up – apart from those in reserved occupations of course. John Sweetland discovered the frustrations of the situation for himself, writing:

> I felt that whatever work I was fortunate to take up would only be of a temporary nature as I would be marking time for two years before being called up for the forces. Prospective employers shared this view too. At the time, the ruling principal for work was to secure a steady job with a pension at the end. In other words, a job for life, which proved difficult in wartime.

Sweetland applied for a job with the customs and excise office, but was amazed to receive a response from the War Office, calling him in for an interview. 'Somehow the Powers That Be had recognised my worth', he wrote, believing that his interest in maps and plotting routes had made him stand out. Fresh in a new CC41 suit, purchased with clothing coupons from his father's outfitters, Messrs Horne and Sons on the corner of Oxford Street and Tottenham Court Road, the 16-year-old presented himself at the Metropole Buildings in Northumberland Avenue at the appointed hour the following week. After passing a written test and completing a successful interview with a rather attractive young lady – 'it was obvious that the thick application of Brylcreem to my hair had tipped the scales in my favour' – the young Sweetland became a temporary civil servant at the Directorate of Labour.

The 'D. Lab', as it was known, was situated in offices on the third floor of Kinnaird House on the corner of Cockspur Street and Haymarket. Sweetland's job, which he called both easy and boring, was to deal with the movements of officers in the Pioneers Corps, updating indexes and rolls as they moved around. Essentially, it was his job to know where all the officers were at any one time. Some of his new colleagues were former military men who had been removed from frontline services after suffering severe injury 'which quite often showed in the form of a disability or nerves'. One such office-mate was a 'wiry corporal' from the Durham Light Infantry, who was injured after capturing an Italian soldier in the Western Desert campaign. Sweetland wrote:

> The two lay on the sand taking cover, the corporal with legs apart and both hands on his Bren gun, concentrated on any enemy movement ahead, the Italian by his side. Suddenly, the prisoner jumped up and ran as fast as his legs could carry him having dropped a small, short-fused grenade known as a Red Devil between the corporal's legs. Despite the shock and pain he shuffled around and, as he said, shot at him 'till bits blew off'. Details of his injuries were not divulged to me but he did say that one aspect of his forthcoming marriage was worrying him.

The young Sweetland also had to learn how to deal with office politics, especially in the case of two civilian workers who were prone to falling out with each other: 'This made things awkward for me as I was constantly questioned by both as to what one had said about the other.'

Bunty's schooling came to an abrupt halt when her school was evacuated to the country south of London. Aged 15, she refused to leave, so stayed at home with her parents. Whenever evacuation was mentioned she resolutely rejected the idea of leaving. 'I wanted to stay with my home and parents and everything I knew,' she said. There were several more evacuations during the war once the action started getting heavy. Some young people would find themselves bound abroad on ships crossing the Atlantic towards Canada. More than 211,000 applications had been made to the Children's Overseas Reception Board (CORB) by July 1940, so many in fact, that the board said it could accept no more.

The scheme came to a swift and tragic end, however, on 17 September that year, when the SS *City of Benares*, a steam passenger ship, was torpedoed by a German U-boat about 250 miles west-southwest off Rockall. The boat took about half-an-hour to sink. Seventy-three of the vessel's ninety child evacuees were killed, along with numerous other passengers and crew. One evacuee, who did survive, later recounted his tale, which was subsequently published in *Forgotten Voices of the Second World War*.

Colin Ryder-Richardson recalled two loud bangs and then the smell of cordite. Dressed in pyjamas, slippers and a life jacket, he made his way to the top deck where he was helped onto a lifeboat by a nurse. He wrote:

> It was freezing cold and the boat was waterlogged, to make things worse there was a force ten gale. I clung on to the nurse, then as the night went on, lots of people were dying. This man on the boat gently suggested to me that I should release the nurse as, in his view, she was dead.

Even after realising his closest companion was now a corpse, Colin found himself unable to let go of her. It would have been cruel he said, still clinging on to hope that they would soon be rescued and she could be saved. Eventually nature did the job for him, the nurse was swept away in the storm. Another student started drinking seawater to quench his thirst, and subsequently dived into the water. The survivors spent eight days in a life raft in the Atlantic before being rescued. By that point, CORB had sent 2,664 abroad, but, following the deaths of the *City of Benares* children, it was decided not to risk sending any more evacuees by sea. So many ended up in the countryside or simply stayed at home, as Bunty did: 'I felt that I would only worry more about my family and home if I couldn't be there with them, and I'm glad I stayed.'

Chapter Three

Working Through the War

For older teens and young adults, war meant work. By June 1944, more than half of Britain's twenty-two-million-strong labour force was engaged in some form of war work, twenty-two per cent in the armed services and thirty-three per cent in civilian roles. There were some 1.5 million people unemployed in 1939. By 1945, that number was 54,000.

As Angus Calder points out, however, the true number of people engaged in some form of war-related work was much higher when you factor-in part-timers – volunteers who were older than the retirement age and children younger than employment age. Then there were those whose day job was not linked to the war, but who volunteered to be part of the Home Guard or firewatchers in their free time.

On the day that war was declared, parliament passed the National Service (Armed Forces) Act, which conscripted all males aged between 18 and 41 into the war effort. The call-up had begun. In December 1941, the upper age limit was raised to 51. In September 1939, there were some 897,000 people in the British army, a number that had almost doubled to 1,656,000 just nine months later. There were exemptions, most notably for those who were not medically fit enough, and others working in certain trades that were deemed vital to keep the war-machine's engine running.

Some five-million men were classified as being in a reserved occupation and therefore exempt – initially at least – from the call-up. These included the miners who dug up the fuel and materials needed in war, the farmers and agricultural workers growing the nation's food, bakers who fed the citizens, and doctors and other medical staff who treated the sick and did their best to keep the population healthy. Engineering was one of the industries with the highest number of exemptions, so important was it to the war effort. According to Norman Ferguson in *The Second World War: A Miscellany*, other reserved occupations included ambulance and train drivers, fishermen, lighthouse keepers, prison warders, teachers, trade union officials and saxophone makers.

Those not in reserved occupations, however, were in line for the call-up. By 1945, about a quarter of men under the age of 50 were in the services. Some, such as those who opposed the war on religious, political or pacifist grounds, could apply for conscientious-objector (CO) status. According to the Peace Pledge Union's online CO Project, and accompanying book *Refusing to Kill*, almost 60,000 people were classified as conscientious objectors during the Second World War. A further 18,495 had their applications to be placed on the CO register rejected. Those who refused to carry out the work they were now legally obliged to do were fined, and those who refused to pay the fines were jailed.

There were three grades of conscientious objector, or 'conshie', as they became known by the public, as determined by a tribunal chaired by a county court judge. The first was where applicants could be given unconditional CO status. The second grade was that of registered conditional, which meant they were exempted from the call-up as long as they did useful civilian work. The third grade was to be awarded non-combatant status. This meant that they had to join the army, but would not be required to handle weapons. They would instead serve in units such as the Medical Corps, the specially formed Non-Combatants Corps, or perform administrative roles. The decision on whether or not to enlist was obviously a highly charged and thought-provoking one, no more so than for the young people who had heard of the horrors and heroism that their fathers faced in the First World War.

Writing for the *Mass Observation* project, one 18-year-old civil servant from Highams Park faced just such a dilemma. On 4 January 1940, he wrote in his diary that he had attended a pacifism meeting, after which he got into a heated debate with three army recruits while on his way home. He felt that he had won his argument and was determined that, should the call-up come his way, he would refuse to go.

The following day, however, his decision was faltering. His father faced losing his job, the teenager wrote, which would mean he and his brother would need to contribute more money to the family's purse. To become a conscientious objector would most likely lead to him losing his job as many employers sacked those not willing to support the war effort. While noting the ill feeling felt by many towards those who objected to war work, the young civil servant questioned how fair it would be on his parents for him to suddenly stop bringing in a salary.

Eventually, the teenager concluded that he had a year to consider the problem, and hoped that he would not have to make a decision anyway as the war could be over by Christmas. According to his later entries for the *Mass Observation* project, the 18-year-old ended up working for the meteorological branch of the Royal Navy a year or so later. For others, however, there was little debate to be had. Another *Mass Observation* participant decided, after some deliberation and arguments with his parents, not to wait for his call-up papers, and instead volunteered himself for the army.

The 19-year-old who lived on Sugden Road in southwest London, was a student at Emmanuel College in Cambridge when war commenced. But, even before the declaration of war, his intentions were clear. On Tuesday, 29 August, he wrote of a meeting in the street with his former history master. The teacher quizzed him about his intentions, to which the student replied that he would sign up. His former master concluded that that was probably for the best as it saved any arguing over the matter.

As for many of his age, the frustration at a lack of activity grew until he could take it no more, forcing him to make the decision to sign himself up rather than wait for the official summons. Efforts to join the Air Raid Precautions had been rejected due to his being of military age, which also made it a struggle finding a decent job. Who, after all, would want to employ a young man who at any time could be called away to fight for his country? Despite the entreaties of his parents and other older family members and friends, who implored him to wait until he was actually called up rather than to volunteer to join the war, he submitted an application for a military commission.

So it was that on 4 October 1939, just a month and a day since war had been declared, the eager young man found himself going through a selection process in Cambridge to join the services. He writes a very full and engaging account of his sign-up day in his diary. He was one of sixty or so young men to be first interviewed by a board of people, which comprised both military and civilian representatives. He was questioned – not unpleasantly so – about his ambitions and attributes. Having a decent grasp of German and French stood him in good stead, while his basic knowledge of trigonometry was enough to secure him a place in the Royal Artillery.

The keen recruit was then sent into another room where he had to fill out various forms in triplicate before moving onto a medical. Having removed his shirt, he was seen by four different medical professionals, who noted down on yet more forms such personal details as his physique, general health, and the colour of his eyes and hair.

Then, finally, came the swearing-in ceremony. On one of the numerous forms he had filled in he had said he was an agnostic. The swearing-in officer asked if, despite the applicant's far-from-committed view of God and Christianity, he would mind swearing the oath on the Bible anyway, as this would save a lot of extra hassle. The obliging student said he did not mind, especially after he was told the Holy Book would be open at one of its ruder parts: Ezekiel Chapter 23, a tale of two prostitutes. Having been sworn in, the new trainee officer received two-shillings pay, with a little extra to cover the cost of his fare. So it was, several hours after entering as a student, he emerged a fully signed-in and sworn-up member of the armed services.

Away from the military, the government relied on people to do war work. By 1944, a third of the country's population, including some seven-million women, were engaged in war work. In March 1941, the minister of labour, Ernest Bevin, introduced the Essential Work Order. This required all skilled workers to register, while barring those in certain professions, such as mining, munitions and agriculture, from leaving their professions.

It became a criminal offence to even be late for work, as one 20-year-old apprentice driller found to his cost in 1942. The lad had been between a quarter- and half-an-hour late for work forty-seven times in sixty-five days. He was sentenced to a month's hard labour. The magistrates lamented the fact that he was in a protected trade, saying the 'proper place' for him would be in the army where he could learn discipline.

Most people, however, took their responsibility seriously. For young women, war opened up a lot of options that would previously have been closed to them. As during the First World War, with many of the men away fighting, it fell on women to make up the gap in the domestic workforce. Initially, only single women aged between 25 and 30 were called upon to do war work, but by 1943 almost ninety per cent of single women and eighty per cent of married ones were engaged in some activity.

Jobs ranged from factory work to farming in the government's Women's Land Army. Many also joined the military services, carrying out duties such as driving and engineering. The future Queen Elizabeth II famously became a mechanic and driver for the Auxiliary Territorial Service when she was a 19-year-old princess and first in line for the throne. Her father and the government had initially decided not to allow her to join up, saying her place was to prepare for life as the head of state, but she insisted and eventually got her way. Although she carried on living in the royal palaces, between 10.00 am and 5.00 pm each day she worked in garages and drove trucks. 'One of her major joys was to get dirt under her nails and grease stains on her hands, and display these signs of labour to her friends', wrote Irving Wallace in an article for the American magazine *Collier's* in March 1947.

As well as the official work, many volunteered for various causes, for example men for the Home Guard or Air Raid Precautions, and women for the Women's Institute (WI) or Women's Voluntary Service (WVS). The latter organisation, in particular, played a huge role in organising the evacuation of children, and providing food, water and assistance to those bombed out of their homes. However, it wasn't just their time that people were willing to give up – money was also often relinquished for the war effort. War was an expensive business, and by December 1940, it was costing £10 million a day, of which about half had to be borrowed from the public.

In her diary, Bunty mentions going to a 'Wings for Victory' gathering in Trafalgar Square. As an interesting aside, although not the centre of the City of London, Trafalgar Square is the centre of Greater London, as it is the point from which all distances from the capital are measured. To be precise, the exact point is next to a statue of a mounted King Charles I at the south side of the square, which was the site of the original Charing Cross. Wings for Victory was a week-long fundraising drive hoping to generate about £150 million. It was a national event, but the centrepiece was a Lancaster bomber on display in Trafalgar Square.

The opening event was attended by several thousand people. British Pathé News reported that it was the largest gathering of people in London since the coronation of King George VI on 12 May 1937. As part of the opening ceremony, 1,300 pigeons were released to carry messages to the 1,300 fundraising committees around the country.

One of the busiest professions in wartime London was that of the firefighter. Not all of the bombs the Luftwaffe dropped over London were designed to explode – many were simply meant to start fires. And they were incredibly effective. One firefighter, Frederick Delve, said the Luftwaffe timed their raids for when the Thames was at its lowest tide. 'It was only possible for fire boats to be right in the centre of the river and for firemen to take hoses ashore it would mean them standing up to their shoulders in mud to struggle ashore with lines of hose', he wrote in his memoirs published by Max Arthur in *Forgotten Voices of the Second World War*.

Many men and machines were therefore needed to battle the blazes. The professionals were joined by volunteers from the Auxiliary Fire Service, and firewatchers who stood at tall vantage points to observe where fires broke out. It was the efficiency of the firewatchers at St Paul's Cathedral that meant incendiary devices landing near Christopher Wren's masterpiece could be quickly doused with sand before they caused any major damage. The survival of St Paul's, relatively unscathed, was one of the great morale-boosting tales for the British public to enjoy. Apparently, Winston Churchill had issued orders that the cathedral was to be saved at all costs, such was the importance of its symbolic survival.

Before September 1939, there were 1,850 fire pumps in the whole of Britain. By the end of December that year, London alone had some 2,300. Just getting to blazes could be a challenge for the fire service. As Angus Calder notes, they had to navigate around 'diversion signs, over craters and debris, past dangling telephone and trolley bus wires, over the carpet of splintered glass and through cordons of people who begged them to stop and save their homes'.

Once they got to the scene, there was danger in fighting the flames. Almost 820 firemen and women lost their lives across Britain, with a further 7,000 more seriously injured. Many more suffered some form of exhaustion brought on by the punishing forty-eight-hour shifts, which were followed by twenty-four-hour breaks.

As well as the risk of smoke inhalation or being trapped by collapsing buildings, they also feared being blinded, either temporarily or permanently, by sparks or just the intense heat. Firefighters from other parts of the country would travel to help, but there were reports of them finding themselves utterly useless as their hoses did not have the correct fittings to attach to the hydrants. Very quickly, though, such errors were corrected, as a more coherent national service emerged from the 1,666 locally organised brigades. 'The reorganisation was completed with remarkable speed', Calder wrote, 'an efficient organisation was shaped from a chaos of petty interests. Such things were possible in total war.'

The last night of the Blitz – 10 May 1941 – proved to be one of the worst for the firefighters in London, however, as a low River Thames left them with depleted water stocks. Fires burned across London, stretching from Romford in the east to Hammersmith in the west, the bombers having been aided by a bright and clear moon. Some 1,436 people were killed, setting a new record for one night's raid. A further 1,792 were seriously injured. London Tower, the mint, War Office, courts and Westminster Abbey were all hit. About 250,000 books at the British Museum and £100,000 worth of gin on City Road were destroyed by fire. In that one night, London was battered by 2,200 fires, one third of its streets were rendered impassable, and every railway station, bar one, was blocked for weeks. Some 155,000 families were left without water, electricity or gas, not to mention the many who were left homeless. Firefighters spent eleven days putting out the fires.

Then there were those whose job it was to repair as best they could the damage done by the bombs. The government, in late 1944, formed the

London Repairs Executive. Over the following six months, some 800,000 homes had been brought back to a tolerable standard, and by 1947, two years after the war, the vast majority of bomb-damaged homes were once again habitable.

For Bunty, meanwhile, the war meant several different professions. She started working in a bank – the only woman in an office of men – and recalls spending air raids sheltering in the building's safe-room. She then followed her vocation to become a physiotherapist. Once again, the war meant she was not short of work as plenty of people required treatment. She writes of several in her diary, from those who had injured various limbs to a nineteen-year-old chap who had attempted suicide and suffered severe bouts of depression. Bunty's war therefore revolved around helping and healing those hurt by the conflict.

Chapter Four

The Reality of Air Raids

T
he defining images of the Second World War in London are those depicting the damage caused by the Blitz, a series of bombing raids carried out by the German Luftwaffe on the city. The first bombers attacked London between 11.20 pm and about 12.30 am on the night of 25 August 1940. It was dramatic, but a mere glimpse of what was to come. Only nine people were killed and fifty-eight hospitalised.

The worst period of the war for London began between 5.00 pm and 6.00 pm in the afternoon of Saturday, 7 September 1940. About 300 bombers, supported by 600 single-seater fighter planes, attacked the city. East London, in particular, bore the brunt of the bombs. A further 150 bombers returned three hours later, the waves of attacks continuing until about 4.30 am on the Sunday morning.

More than 1,000 fires were started, 3 train stations rendered useless, and 430 people killed, with a further 1,600 seriously injured. So began the Blitz. There was a raid every night for the next fifty-seven days, with an average of 200 planes taking part in each attack.

People had been prepared. Before war had even been declared they knew the conflict was coming, and with it would come air raids. German airships, generally referred to as Zeppelins – even though only some of them were made by the company of that name – had attacked Britain from above during the First World War. Such attacks were followed by the Gotha and Zeppelin-Staaken bombers. The damage was meagre when compared with what was to come in the Second World War. The effect, however, was significant, as it showed that Britain was on the front line. Some 1,413 people were killed (600 in London) in about 100 raids across the country during the First World War, a fraction of those who would die in the Blitz. It was proof Britain was in the firing line.

So when the Second World War loomed, the politicians and population knew German aircraft would be crossing the seas to attack Britain directly. The government predicted that the first night alone would claim some 58,000 lives. It became a common topic of conversation for the country's residents. One 19-year-old *Mass Observer* diarist noted how he and his girlfriend discussed the imminent arrival of enemy aircraft. She said she would prefer to be killed straight away rather than survive mutilated.

Air-raid sirens blared out soon after war was declared, but it would not be until August 1940, that they would be sounded in earnest. Shortly after hearing first the air-raid siren, then the all-clear on Sunday 3 September, 1939, the 19-year-old *Mass Observer* contributor expressed a view that, surprisingly, was seemingly shared by many – when would the action start? It would be several months before raiders started attacking. The interlude became known as the 'Phony War', or the 'Bore War'. If they were to be attacked, better just to get on with it.

Though there were numerous raids throughout the war, they can be broadly drawn into three distinct phases. These were the Blitz between September 1940 and May 1941; the 'baby' Blitz that consisted of fourteen nights of bombing between January and April 1944; and finally the V-weapon attacks between June 1944 and March 1945.

Geoffrey Dellar was a teenager living in Croydon when the war began. Between August 1940 and his joining the RAF in February 1944, he kept a diary documenting his experience of the air raids. His ten notebooks are stored at the Imperial War Museum in London and are a fairly comprehensive but non-emotional account of the raids he lived through. One such entry from close to the beginning of the Blitz offers an insight into life on the ground as battle took place in the skies.

In the entry Dellar wrote:

> This afternoon at 13:00 hrs I again heard wave after wave of bombers coming over towards London, although I was unable to see them.
>
> A few seconds later the alert was sounded and we all went into the dining room, as we have no air-raid shelter. A few seconds after this more bombers approached, pursued by RAF fighters, and soon a dog-fight was in progress. After a while the AA (Anti-Aircraft) guns joined in and the explosions grew so heavy that we were obliged to take whatever additional shelter our hall offered. The house was shaken by a long succession of shell-bursts and the fight was by now practically directly overhead with machine guns rattling viciously and the noise of diving planes growing louder with every second. However, the fight gradually passed over to the south once more and, after only a few minutes only RAF fighter patrols were about. The raiders passed [signal] was given at approximately 14:00 hrs. Some of the bombers used in the raid were seen to be

Heinkels (IIIK). A second warning was given today at 17.45 hrs and several fighter patrols were about; but no enemy planes came near and the all-clear was given at 18.10 hrs.

Dellar's diaries are full of detailed notes on raids, although they offer few of his feelings about such experiences. Friday, 13 September 1941, proved unlucky for two men in a house on Station Road near the site of a bomb strike. Dellar wrote:

At 22.55 we heard several bombs whistling down and learned later that they had dropped in West Wickham. They had fallen in a straight line across West Wickham starting in Beckenham Road with intermediate bombs in Ravenswood Crescent, where a gas main was blown open in the roadway; in Ravenswood Avenue where several houses were damaged; in Braemar Gardens where other houses were damaged and finishing with one on Riches, a furniture shop on the corner Braemar Gardens and the High Street.

Only two men were involved in it, one of them being killed immediately and the other dying on the way to hospital. A small crater about four or five feet across was found in Devonshire Way after the raid. It may have been a small bomb but was more probably an AA shell which had failed to explode until reaching the ground.

Two days later, Dellar writes about another fairly typical day that saw four air-raid warnings, two fifteen-minute-long dogfights, one bomber shot down, and then an all-night raid which, though consisting of 'gun fire', 'AA guns' and 'whistling bombs', was not as heavy as previous attacks.

The aftermath of air raids also left an impression on the young Dellar. On Saturday, 8 March 1941, he was driven through London to Hertfordshire. He wrote of the scenes he saw in the area of Kensington Park Road:

The road was strewn with glass and smashed window frames. Tiles were missing from the roofs of all the houses, and from one window a big Union Jack was already fluttering. A woman was standing in the street in a dressing gown, smiling up to somebody else in one of the damaged houses, and all round her men were busy clearing the glass away.

The next new piece of damage we saw was just on the south side of London Bridge where there was a big crater in the road. Heaps of glass were piled up in the gutters and all around the crater were wooden blocks thrown up from the road. Men were already working there with electric drills and others were mending the pipes below the surface. Then as we reached the north side of London Bridge we saw that three streets had been roped off owing to an unexploded bomb.

An insurance building on the corner of one of them was damaged, pieces of the stone having been chipped off round the doorway. As we went on we saw police on duty at every street corner and when we approached Liverpool Street Station we found that this was also roped off. As we came home a different way we found the reason for this. Along Bishopgate several bombs had been dropped, two of which penetrated to a subway which may have been part of the underground railway. There were several big holes in the wall of the station and a police station opposite Liverpool Street Station had also been hit.

On the wall of the police station was a notice-board with what appeared to be a list of casualties which was being anxiously scanned by a small number of people. A fire-engine was still outside the station (this was at about 6.30 hrs) and hoses were only just being rolled up. We saw only one bomb in North London, this being one which fell in Kingsland Road. The only damage it did was to hoardings on the side of the road.

Dellar returned to London later that day, where he made these observations:

On the way home through London there were few people about. The roads on the north side of London Bridge were still closed and as we got further south we saw people hurrying along to the tube stations carrying sacks which probably contained bedding. Other people were going down into the underground shelters although it was only about half-past six and not yet dark.

On the corner of Milkwood Road and Jessop Road another house had been hit and workmen were still clearing debris from the road when we came home. At Woodside a road was closed owing to the raid, but after that nothing else was seen. Afterwards several things were discovered about the raid, as follows. The three roads roped off on the north side of London Bridge were closed because of about twelve DA (Delayed Action) bombs which had fallen on Saturday night. One was in the Customs House at the bottom of Harp Lane, another in Minning Home and others in Fenchurch Street and around that district.

A HE (High Explosive) bomb was dropped on Nestlé's milk building in Eastcheap in which was a police station. Four constables and a superintendent's daughter were killed. The Cafe de Paris in the West End was also hit by a bomb, several dancers were killed and a large number of the band, including the leader Ken Johnson.

Writer Virginia Woolf, who had a home on Mecklenburgh Square, also recorded the destruction she saw on Tuesday, 10 September 1940:

The house about thirty yards from ours struck at one in the morning by a bomb ... completely ruined. [Another house] ... still smoldering, a great pile of bricks. Underneath all the people who had gone down to their shelter. Scraps of cloth hanging to the bare walls at the side still standing. A looking glass I think swinging. Like a tooth knocked out – a clean cut.

Another young Londoner's diary, also held by the Imperial War Museum, does give a flavour of what it was like living through an air raid. Joyce Wiener wrote on 16 April 1940:

Wednesday night here was quite unbelievable. You know we have experienced nearly all the big raids that there have been, have, indeed, had eight months or so of it and really are as hardened as anyone can become, but this shook us to our marrow. The alert went quite early and I said 'they mean business' which was quite obvious no later than five minutes afterwards. Masses and masses of planes could be heard – all flying so low that it sounded as if they were about to land – they gave you the impression that they were flying wing tip to wing tip, covering the sky so that there was no portion of it left clear of them.

A sea of droning was above and below you and all the time these thundering, bellowing guns rent the air with no success at all in lessening the all-pervading hum. I went to bed – I always do, and I was confident that I would soon fall asleep. It was absolutely impossible that night. Each crashing thud blew back the thick satin curtains in my room – flashes like sheet lightning followed each crash. The porters running hither and thither outside reported huge glares in the sky and the sound of fire bells was a ceaseless accompaniment all the endless night.

The grinding sound of bombs as they touched the earth shook the basement floor and shook your heart nearly out of your body too, as the whistle came down each time you thought as you had not thought for months 'this one is for you'. I exhausted all the prayers and all the Psalms I knew and I found relief in swearing each time a bomb came down and we were still alive. It was a night of unbelievable horror and it just would not end. As in the beginning, we waited exhausted for the dawn.

It was a shattered world that woke in sunlight. As this city takes hiding after hiding its majesty becomes more and more apparent. The damage is now, alas, linking up and areas not mere corners now have taken the knock. 'Where, ere you walk' could be savagely parodied in this terrible devastation and somehow these damaged buildings have a beauty and significance in ruin that they never had whole. It just is that we didn't love them enough I think. I don't want to dwell on the people but the stories are heart-rending. All day long the stories poured into the office and we were shaken to the roots by what we heard. That was Thursday. By today and really by Friday London had picked itself up and, as the damage and havoc were greater, so indeed are the insouciance and the rebound.

Of course, even when the bombs had stopped falling from the sky, they did not stop being a threat. Even today, unexploded bombs are found in London – leftovers from the Second World War – sparking road closures, police cordons and visits from the army's explosives experts. In the war, unexploded bombs, or UXBs, were regular finds for the people of London.

In his 1948 book *Red Roses Every Night*, an account of how the war affected cinemas in the city, Guy Morgan recounts one such discovery. A 2,000lb bomb, one of the largest to be dropped on London, was discovered in an empty shop across the road from the main entrance to the Granada Cinema in Woolwich. It was unearthed eighteen months after being dropped. A family had been sleeping above it for a year and thousands walked passed it every day blissfully unaware of the threat slumbering a few feet below them.

Jonathan Sweetland was 14 when the Blitz began. By the end of the first week, he and his fellow Londoners were 'becoming accustomed to the sirens and spasmodic night attacks'. He wrote:

I found my experiences exciting. After all, it was just like watching a film, only happening to other people with me as a spectator from our balcony vantage point outside our front door. The sounds of the blitz were distinctive.

Sometimes we would be made aware that raiders were on their way as the BBC radio programmes suddenly became indistinct, bringing on a very unwelcome anticipation. Soon then, the first siren would be heard, perhaps away in the distance. Then others would join sounding nearer and nearer until our very own siren on the roof of Albany Street Police Station would join in. The guns too had their different sounds. Our local battery on Primrose Hill would let out a thunderous roar and sometimes a mobile gun stopped in Cumberland Market would let fly with a tremendous bang.

The soft crumps of exploding anti-aircraft shells were mild, accompanied by the falling shrapnel which gave out metallic rings as pieces hit the hard ground or bounced off or rolled along roofs before it too pinged to the ground. A shower of incendiaries sounded like a hundred cricket balls struck by bats, and as for falling bombs, sometimes a long, drawn out whistle, but a close one would give an ever increasing rushing sound.

He later called the sound of the sirens the 'nightmare chorus'.

In 1944, a new kind of bomb was being dropped on London – incendiaries with delayed timers, set to go off about three minutes after impact, or to put it another way, just as a brave Londoner was standing over it attempting to extinguish it with sand. Their bodies were 'riddled with white hot steel and burning magnesium', Sweetland, now 16, wrote.

The device had proved very successful as we watched lifeless and injured residents being carried away. The air was filled with the smell of burning houses, hot metal and the reek of cordite; and everywhere underfoot bomb and shell splinters with small craters about two feet in diameter and three feet deep where an incendiary had exploded.

After one such raid, Sweetland had his first up-close experience with a fatal victim of the war. While running down a passageway to find a fire alarm, he noticed a dark liquid on the concrete floor:

Shining my torch to the left the beam picked out a pair of legs stiffly stuck out in front of me. Avoiding the pool of blood I stopped in horror, hardly daring to move the torch beam upwards from the legs. My horror increased. This was the body of a middle-aged woman who had caught the full blast of an incendiary in the stomach of which there was little left. She must have died instantly. I quickly looked away. This was the first war victim I had seen in close up. Sickened, and with a pounding heart, I walked from the dark passageway into the pink light of Cumberland Market where I found a constable watching the fire to whom I reported my discovery. Eventually I was given her name, a married woman with two children.

Later in the war, Londoners had to face the V-1 flying bombs. The V stood for *Vergeltung*, German for retribution. According to a German propaganda radio broadcast, the use of the V-1 was 'to arouse expectation among our friends and terror among the enemy that there are intensifications to follow'. The barrage balloons that had stood guard over the city centre were moved to the south to form an aerial frontier. Though he understood the need for the balloons to be moved, John Sweetland noted that their absence gave him a feeling of 'unprotected nakedness overhead'.

The 'Doodlebugs', as they came to be known, were launched from the French coast. Targeted at Tower Bridge, their direction was controlled by an autopilot system. Each was fitted with an 850 kg warhead designed to explode upon impact. The first arrived on 13 June 1944, striking a railway bridge on Grove Road in Mile End, killing six people and injuring another nine. The main V-1 offensive ran until 5 September 1944.

'The approach of a V-1 could be heard from some way off and was described as sounding like a motorbike or car struggling to climb uphill', wrote Laurence Ward in *Bomb Damage Maps*. They could come over at any time and the damage they caused was soon mounting up and creating backlogs for those trying to repair London's homes.

Terence O'Brien wrote in *Civil Defence*:

Three weeks after these attacks began there was a backlog of 194,000 houses awaiting repairs; over 20,000 were being damaged each day and in spite of a labour force of 33,000 men, arrears were mounting at the rate of 6,000 houses a day.

The plus side was that they were easily spotted and followed, meaning emergency services could reach the crash sites in relatively quick time. According to Laurence Ward, some 10,000 V-1s were launched at London during the war, with about 2,368 hitting the city. 'A high number succumbed to mechanical failure', he wrote, 'and of those that did reach the UK, many either fell short of their intended target or were brought down by barrage balloons and the RAF.'

Britain's aerial-defence network was also pretty effective at stopping the flying bombs. Of the first 4,000 that were launched, 1,270 of them actually reached London. Of these, according to Basil Collier in *A Short History of the Second World War* 1,241 were destroyed by the British defences. Over the following weeks, a further 2,222 out of 3,791 missiles were destroyed. On one particular day, ninety out of ninety-seven were dealt with by the defence teams, which included ground-based gunners, fighter-planes and the barrage balloons.

The second phase of V-1 attacks took place between 14 September 1944 and 12 January 1945, followed by a third, final flurry, from 3–29 March 1945. Over both periods, however, the total number launched was less than 1,500, with only 97 actually reaching the London area. A further fifty were targeted at Manchester, but only one actually made it that far.

Sweetland said he had eleven near misses from the Doodlebugs. 'As the nights became longer so the number of V-1s increased, that indescribable engine noise, perhaps like a motorised raspberry blowing through a motorbike exhaust.'

On one occasion, he and his girlfriend were walking across Kensington Gardens on their way to a concert at the Royal Albert Hall. Sweetland writes:

> Then, in the distance, came that engine noise, coming closer and closer. As the engine cut out we stopped to shelter under a tree as though it were raining, for all the good that would do. Fortunately we stood on the correct side of the trunk, which was rather large, for although the explosion wasn't too close the blast shot past us taking a shower of leaves from the tree as it went.

Other times he could see them from his home:

> I could stand in our open doorway looking over to the east. I would pick out the bright yellow/orange pinpoint of light from the motor's exhaust which slowly grew ever larger, tracing a straight line towards me, bringing back the helpless dartboard feeling of the blitz. Mother would remain trembling inside the flat while I would be rooted to the spot, mentally imploring the engine not to cut out. Occasionally two bombs would approach, halving our chances of survival. Side by side, the bombs would steadily come closer, the gap between them slowly widening as if to say 'well if he doesn't get you, I will'.

This was followed by the fear of hearing the engine stop, meaning the bomb was about to fall: 'From the shattering exhaust noise to immediate silence, except for the increasing wind noise as the bomb gathered velocity on its downward path to its target.'

Then, on 8 September 1944, came the larger V-2s, which were launched from the Netherlands. Again, Sweetland had something of a close shave:

> One evening I left Kinnaird house, crossing as usual to Cockspur Street. Just before I reached the bus stop there came a tremendous over-head explosion which made me nearly jump out of my skin. Up in the clear blue sky was a large, round, white cloud, preceded by a curving vapour trail. Following the explosion came the rumbling noise of the rocket's descent through the sky, the V-2 had exploded in flight.

In 1945, in the final throes of the war, Sweetland's relaxation in his bedroom was interrupted by an 'almighty blue and white flash followed by an explosion' from a few streets away. He set out to see where the V-2 had crashed and found it had landed on a tabernacle on Tottenham Court Road.

> The spectacle provided me with the most eerie and chilling sight of the war. The building had totally collapsed and the rubble was spectacularly lit by searchlights provided, I assumed, by the Americans who swarmed over the site assisting the civil defence workers. Naturally the traffic was diverted away from the scene so the silence, broken only by the mobile generator feeding the lights and the sharp sounds of picks and shovels striking the rubble, added to the eeriness. The scene, lit against the backdrop of a dark sky, had the unreality of a film set. The power of the V-2 was awesome.

About 1,400 V-2s were launched at London between September 1944 and March 1945, with 517 finding their target, killing 2,511 people and seriously injuring a further 5,869.

Basil Collier, in reference to both the V-1 and V-2, says:

> In the whole course of the campaign about 9,000 civilians were killed or seriously injured by long-range rockets. Many buildings were destroyed or damaged but no objective of outstanding military importance was affected.

Being prepared for the air aids was vital. Bunty's father had fortified their basement with wooden pillars, using tricks and techniques he learned in the trenches during the First World War. The government, meanwhile, issued numerous leaflets and posters to help people get as ready as possible for what was to come. Air-raid wardens carried out surveys of homes in their areas so they would know who lived in each particular house or flat. This would prove invaluable to locate those who might be missing in the event of a bomb strike. Householders were told to inform their warden of any visitors they might have, and to also advise them if they planned to vacate their properties.

Knowing where you were going to go for shelter was a key priority. When the air-raid siren, nicknamed the 'Wailing Willie', 'Wailing Winnie', or the 'Wobbler', sounded – a high-pitched, two-minute long, rising and falling noise, often followed by shrill blasts from a policeman's or warden's whistle – shelter should be sought.

'It is unlikely that you will have more than seven minutes to complete your arrangements', advised one leaflet issued in the City of Westminster, 'so make sure they are ready before there is an air-raid. Do not remain in the street – take cover'.

Hand rattles would be sounded if there was a gas attack, being the cue to don gas masks and seek shelter. A further two-minute long, continuous, steady note of a siren would denote the raids had passed. Where a hand rattle had been used, a hand bell would signify all was clear and that there was no lingering gas. The Ministry of Health issued leaflets advising on first aid, warning citizens that they may see unpleasant things. 'Be prepared to see severe wounds,' read the leaflet, 'Be courageous and keep your head. Keep your mind on your duty to save your injured fellow man.'

People were advised to carry several clean handkerchiefs or small towels to be used as bandages, with the 'first and most important duty' of anyone finding a casualty being to 'stop bleeding'.

Homeowners were also advised to attach large metal clips onto the end of their broom handles, with which they could pick up and move incendiary devices in an emergency, although the best advice was to leave devices where they were and report them to a warden. The minister of home security ordered all lofts to be decluttered of furniture and junk, so that they would be clear of anything combustible in the event of a bomb strike. Papers and metal objects were taken away for use in the war effort.

When raids came, there were several options for shelter. A census taken in London in November 1940, found nine per cent of people would take refuge in a public shelter, four per cent in the underground, and twenty-seven per cent in their own home shelters, such as Andersons or Morrisons.

The rest were either out at work or sleeping at home, though often the latter meant in a more sheltered part of the house, such as under the dining room table or in the cupboard beneath the stairs. Some, like Bunty, had a basement in which they could seek refuge.

The public surface shelters were not popular as they were dark and wet, and the limited toilets they had would quickly overflow. Also, a shortage of cement had led to many of these brick structures being put up without any grouting. There were also trenches in the parks, but again these were not favoured by many, due to the mud and water that would collect around residents' feet. Anderson shelters, which were put up in people's gardens, were used, but again they were not popular as they were prone to flooding, were cramped and did nothing to keep out the noise of an air raid.

Some decamped every night to caves in Chislehurst where a small community developed, including a barber shop, concert area and place for church services. There are reports of whole families taking over caves, and even furnishing them with beds and chairs. Back in the city though, one of the most notorious public shelters was to be found in Stepney. It was so significant, that tourists even went there to gawp at it and its occupants. Then there were the Tilbury railway arches, a collection of vaults and cellars that, along with a neighbouring warehouse-loading yard, had been taken over by the local council to be used as a shelter for up to 3,000 people.

In fact, up to 16,000 were estimated to have used it on some nights, many of them of a colourful and questionable character. As previously mentioned, the tube stations also became shelters, despite the government's initial wish to keep them free to facilitate body storage and troop movements. To get around the ban, people would simply buy a train ticket and then not leave the platform.

Eventually, the government officially allowed tube stations to be used. In response to somewhat squalid conditions and overcrowding, around 600,000 bunks were installed at the tube stations in 1941, together with electric fires and/or coal stoves. Some of the larger shelters had permanent wardens to ensure some degree of peace could be maintained, while ensuring undesirable types were kept out.

Meanwhile, of course, the wealthy could shelter in style at places like the Dorchester Hotel, which had turned its Turkish baths into a rather luxurious refuge, complete with eiderdown beds, separated by curtains to offer privacy and discretion. To highlight the discrepancy between these relative dens of luxury and the squalid public shelters such as that at Stepney, Phil Piratin, leader of Stepney Council and a member of the Communist Party, led a delegation of seventy people, including numerous children, from the East End to the Savoy Hotel. The group effectively forced their way into the hotel's shelter where they availed themselves of its comforts, much to the annoyance of the managers, but to the amusement of the waiters who took it upon themselves to serve the newcomers.

In his 1948 memoirs, extracts of which were reproduced by Carol Harris in *Blitz Diary*, Piratin wrote:

> The management was in a dilemma. They urged the police to throw us out, we were able to impress on the manager that any such attempt would meet with some opposition and that some of his guests in the dining room were likely to be disturbed. He agreed to ignore us; that was what we wanted.

The occupation made headlines and prompted the government to address the conditions of the public shelters. In response to fears about heavier bombs that could pierce further into the earth and also to stop the tubes being used for shelter, the government built eight large shelters between 80 and 150 feet below the surface. These shelters, each capable of holding up to 8,000 people, were, however, not completed until after the Blitz, so, apart from during the doodlebug days, they were largely unused.

The bombs posed many perils to Londoners. If they survived the explosion, there was still a real risk they could be cut or skewered by shards of broken glass. The danger of large fires quickly spreading was apparent, and of course delayed-action and unexploded bombs (UXB) meant that even after a raid, Londoners were still in great danger. A nurse working in London said she could always tell where bombs had fallen because of the smell in the air afterwards. Evelyn White, whose memories have been published in *Forgotten Voices of the Second World War*, said, 'We were crossing over to the nurses' home and we could smell burning sugar and fat and we knew the docks had got it.'

'The aim of the air raids was to disrupt the manufacturing, transport and administrative system in London and to demoralize the civilian population and encourage them to sue for peace', wrote Amy Helen Bell in *London Was Ours*. However, they also provided excitement, especially for London's younger residents. 'They were terrible but there was something very exciting about them,' recalled Bunty. 'I wouldn't have wanted to miss being in London at that time.'

Chapter Five

How to Have Fun in Wartime London

There might have been a war on, but people still wanted to go out and enjoy themselves. It was not easy at first though. As soon as war was declared, the government ordered the closure of all cinemas and theatres:

> In view of the great danger involved in the assembly of large numbers of persons in places where it is not feasible to provide adequate protection against the effects of bombs, it has been decided that during the initial stages of a war all theatres, music-halls, cinemas and other places of entertainment shall be closed throughout the country.

Signs were erected, explaining how the cinemas were 'closed until further notice'. One picture house, the Embassy at Notting Hill Gate, helpfully advised customers that the nearest cinema still open was some 239 miles away in Aberystwyth. The reasoning was sound: large groups of people gathered in one place were the last thing you would want during air raids that the authorities were expecting imminently. The closures met with public outcry, however, with many letters of complaint subsequently appearing in the nation's newspapers.

Playwright George Bernard Shaw, at this time an 83-year-old stalwart of the stage, led the protests. In a letter to *The Times* on 5 September, he called closure of the theatres a 'masterstroke of unimaginative stupidity'. He vociferously argued that the need for places of entertainment was as great as ever, with both a nation's morale to maintain and large numbers of soldiers to entertain. He added, 'We have hundreds of thousands of evacuated children to be kept out of mischief and traffic dangers. Are there to be no pictures for them?'

Instead of closing theatres, the playwright said that the 'now all-powerful' authorities should actually be investing in more, and called for all actors, musicians and entertainers to be exempted from 'every form of service except their own all-important professional one'. He concluded, 'What agent of Chancellor Hitler is it who has suggested that we should all cower in darkness and terror "for the duration"?'

Supporters of Mr Shaw also wrote to *The Times*. One said:

> War is not only dangerous but dull and it is as important to keep
> civilians amused as it is to keep them occupied. War work and
> anxiety are exhausting, and for those who have been through the
> last war – and hardly recovered from it – I think as much diversion
> as possible is necessary.

Their protests did not fall on deaf ears.

Realising the importance of public morale – a recurring theme throughout
the war years – the closure order had been rescinded by the government by
15 September, and theatres and cinemas were once again open for business
– and they were popular, incredibly so.

In 1939, about nineteen-million people were going to the cinema each
week. By 1945, this had risen to thirty million. There were at least 4,000
cinemas operating at any one time across the country. During the war, 160
were destroyed, 60 of which were in London, but those that survived carried
on regardless of the risk they faced.

Attendances naturally dropped during the Blitz, but overall, the amount
people were spending on going to the cinema and theatre doubled over the
war years.

'There were always customers for every house and "business as usual"
was the popular cry at that time', wrote Guy Morgan in his 1948-work *Red
Roses Every Night*.

Granada cinemas offered shelter during raids, and would show films and
host sing-alongs throughout the bombings, with staff taking to sleeping at
work to provide longer opening hours for patrons.

By 1946, it was estimated that a third of the population was going to the
pictures at least once a week. In the six months of her diary, Bunty went to
a see a film or play thirty times. On average, she went to a show or the 'flics'
five times a month, or more than once a week. Brief details of the films
she went to see can be found beneath the relevant diary entries. People also
went to the cinema to get the news from a Pathé newsreel, with children's
cartoons shown before each screening.

In August 1939, cinema managers were issued with a memo advising
them on what to do in the event of an air raid during a screening:

> A priority air-raid warning will be given to cinema managers when
> enemy aircraft are sighted over the North Sea. You will not on any

account pass on this priority warning to your audience. You will merely give the warning 'Red Roses' to your staff so that they will be prepared.

In his foreword to Guy Morgan's *Red Roses Every Night*, Herbert Morrison MP, who had served as home secretary, minister of home security, and the man responsible for civil defence, said:

> There were millions who, between long spells of war work and disturbed nights, turned to the cinema for relaxation. The cinemas never let us down. When they were shut it was only because they were too badly damaged to open. Truly the men and women of the cinemas deserved and had the thanks of the public throughout these terrible years.

Guy Morgan himself wrote:

> They queued patiently in the dark when aircraft were droning overhead; they sat through films while the building was rocked by near misses and glass and plaster showered the auditorium, while the film jumped on the screen or the spotlight bounced from the stage to the ceiling; they put out incendiaries in the stalls and went on with the show; they came with rugs and hot-water bottles when the heating failed, and when part of the roof was blown off and the rain came in they moved into a part of the theatre where it was dry; when their homes were hit, they came back the next morning with the bomb-dust still in their hair, and when the cinema was hit they climbed over the rubble in the street to ask when it would re-open.

Between each feature, the audiences were read a small announcement by the cinema managers, telling them what to do in the event of an air raid:

> If ever an air-raid warning is received, the police advise only those within five minutes' walk of their homes to leave. The show will go on for those who remain. We are sure that any who do leave will do so quietly and without fuss. You will realise how important it will be to keep a cool head. We can actually empty this theatre in two-and-a-half minutes if you help.

When raids did come, many sought shelter in the cinemas, often below the circle. Morgan notes that there were numerous sing-alongs and extra showings to keep them entertained as war raged overhead. 'Audiences became curiously conditioned to menace from the air', he wrote, 'The threat of death by bombing was soon generally accepted as a normal risk.' Some cinemas even created dormitories for their staff, thereby allowing them to sleep at work between ever-lengthening shifts.

Of course, all this relied on people actually being able to get to the cinema. The young John Sweetland wrote:

> Our two local cinemas – the Gaumont in Parkway, Camden Town, and the Paramount in Tottenham Court Road – could be easily reached on bright moonlit nights, but became nearly impossible otherwise. The blackout curtailed much evening outdoor activity.

The cinemas also had to comply with blackout measures as well as being limited to putting up just ten posters detailing their programmes, thanks to paper controls. They also lost many of their staff to the call-up and war work; only the chief operator of the projector was exempted.

The number-one cinema song of the war, according to Morgan, was Vera Lynn's *The White Cliffs of Dover*, while audiences preferred films unrelated to the military events in Europe and Africa. The cinema-going public wanted action, colour and comedy, but not whimsical love affairs, and certainly not productions about the war.

'There was too much drama in their daily lives for them to require it on the screen as well', Morgan wrote. The Ministry of Information tried to give them documentaries, but Morgan said people were resistant to them, although much attention was always paid to the newsreels.

Bunty, who was a regular at the cinema, found her taste for films changing during the war. On one occasion, she records going to see a film – sadly she does not give the name – where she notes how her tastes had changed.

'We saw a film which before the war we should have despised for its artificiality, but today we enjoy because it is truly escapist', she wrote.

But she could also be moved by films about the war, in particular the successes for Britain and her allies. On one day, she went to see *Desert Victory*, a documentary made by the Ministry of Information about the Allies' campaign in North Africa against Rommel, including successes at El Alamein and Tripoli. It was, wrote Bunty, 'a film which made me burst with pride for the 8th Army. I don't remember any film before causing in me so much tension.'

The most popular films were epics such as *Gone with the Wind* and Alfred Hitchcock's *Rebecca*, although in 1942 more pictures about the war started making an appearance. It was the era of great actors such as Noel Coward, Laurence Olivier, Greta Garbo and Ivor Novello. Morgan wrote:

> [Cinemas] … have kept our spirit up. They have taken the worst strain off mind and body. No other form of relaxation has been quite so successful in helping people to bear the burdens of fear and loneliness, discomfort and over-exhaustion, anxiety for husbands and sweethearts and sons and little children.

John Sweetland recalled being in a cinema when the air-raid siren sounded, and facing the dilemma: does one make for shelter or stay for the film?

> When the raiders had arrived an announcement was flashed up onto the screen – 'An alert has sounded, but for patrons who wish to stay the performance will continue. Please leave quietly.'
>
> To stay could be nerve-wracking, especially when things became noisy outside. [But] … a very occasional and risky visit to the cinema was a great treat. Home-produced war films being especially popular as well as providing a much needed boost to morale.

American journalist Quentin Reynolds also experienced a raid while watching a film. In his case it was Alfred Hitchcock's adaptation of Daphne Du Maurier's *Rebecca*. In his 1942 work, *The Wounded Don't Cry*, Reynolds wrote:

> The film had only been running about fifteen minutes and the sinister Mrs Danvers had just made her appearance when the sirens sounded. The picture stopped abruptly and the stage was lighted. The manager walked to the centre of the stage and said, 'Enemy aircraft are in the vicinity. Those who wish to leave may get return tickets at the door. There is an air-raid shelter in the cellar, but this is a good strong building and I really think you'll be as well off where you are.'

One of Reynolds's fellow filmgoers was an air-raid warden who had been watching *Rebecca* with his wife and son:

> He said to his wife with resignation: 'I suppose I'd better go, I'll be back soon honey.'

She said, 'How annoying, just when the picture was getting exciting, but I'll remember and tell you everything that happens dear.'

A typical trip to the cinema would involve a main feature film, then a newsreel produced by the likes of Pathé, Paramount or Gaumont British, depending on the cinema. This was followed by a fifteen-minute sing-along accompanied by a Wurlitzer organ, the words projected onto the screen. A second feature film rounded off the event. John Sweetland wrote:

> The organ would rise from a pit to one side of the stage and perform a half swivel to between the audience and the screen. Bathed in constantly changing coloured lights, the organist would first play his or her signature tune followed by a programme of popular and patriotic songs of the day introduced in a friendly manner, along with jokes and breezy chat throughout sending the audience into a fine spirit of anticipation for the main feature.

Newsreels showing good news for the British troops elicited cheers and applause from the cinema audience. On one occasion in 1943, Sweetland's cinema in Camden Town had a special visitor. The actress Barbara Mullen took to the stage and offered to give a kiss to the first man who paid £5 towards the National Savings scheme. Sweetland recalled:

> An embarrassing silence descended on the audience. Mother looked at father out of the corner of her eye but fortunately for him he moved not a muscle, staring straight ahead. Bidding dropped to £4, then £3 and so on until somebody finally agreed to pay five shillings. The manager, now puce and sweating heavily, and perhaps more embarrassed than Miss Mullen, called for a big hand, both leaving the stage to the accompaniment of a loud chord from the organ.

During miserable and chilly winter nights, the cinemas provided welcome relief, cheer and comfort. 'Unfortunately, once out of the cinema and into the cold, dark, night, to stand perhaps for half-an-hour waiting for a bus that might not turn up, the euphoria soon wore off', Sweetland wrote.

Theatres also did their best to stay open, although it was difficult with so many of their staff being taken to war. The call-up saw many young dancers, actors, stage crew and entertainers join the services, leaving gaps behind.

Noel Coward noted the problem in his diary on Tuesday, 7 October 1941, after having lunch at The Ivy with Robert Helpmann, an Australian-born performer who was the lead dancer with the Saddler Wells Ballet from 1933 to 1950.

'Conversation with Bobbie Helpmann about how difficult it is to keep the ballet going with people being called up all the time.' he wrote. 'Thought of Poland, Holland, Czechoslovakia, Norway, Belgium, France etc and felt it was indeed terrible not to be able to keep the ballet going.'

The Opera House at Covent Garden closed for the duration of the war, the only opera house in Europe to close for the entire six years of conflict. It did, however, provide some relief as an occasional dance hall. Dancing became one of the main pastimes for Londoners of all ages, but particularly with its younger inhabitants. Bunty recalls going to several dances during the first six months of 1943, which provided an opportunity to meet members of the opposite sex as well as mingle with one's friends. As well as the privately organised dances, there were large public halls to which people could go.

The Streatham Locarno, for example, could cater for more than 1,000 people at a time, and was regularly full. Quentin Reynolds wrote of his experience in a club in the Berkeley Square area of London during an air raid. Rather than evacuate, the musicians and dancers simply made more noise to drown out the bombers. Reynolds wrote in *The Wounded Don't Cry*:

> The dance floor was crowded. Men were laughing and girls were smiling with their eyes. Faintly, because we were below the street surface and because of the music, I heard the horrible 'crump' sound of bombs falling. They weren't far away, but here in the nightclub none had a thought for bombs.

There were still concerts at venues like the Albert Hall, although its capacity was halved from 10,000 to 5,000 to better provide a quick and safe exit in the event of an air raid.

At home, television output stopped during the war. The BBC replaced its national and local radio stations with the Home Service, a catch-all channel that everyone with a wireless received. The loss of TV would have only affected a handful of people. The BBC had started broadcasting television from Alexandra Palace in north London in 1936, but it had only got as far as rolling it out to Bristol and Hull before the war intervened. Two days before war was declared, the TV service was stopped with little warning, amid fears that the signals it produced could aid enemy invaders. It did not resume again until 3.00 pm on 7 June 1945, but even then it was only for three-and-a-half hours a day, and only available to people living within a thirty-mile radius of Alexandra Palace. By 1947, only 14,000 people had television licences, although its popularity soared from the late 1940s onwards.

The radio was the real source of entertainment in the home, be it from either of the two BBC channels or foreign stations being picked up by the wireless sets. *It's That Man Again*, a comedy show that ran from 1939 to 1949, was one of the big successes, regularly attracting millions of listeners. It even had a movie spin-off, released in 1943. The man in the title was Adolf Hitler and the phrase 'it's that man again' was coined by the *Daily Express*. The show followed comedian Tommy Handley and his character's journey through the absurdities of government and bureaucracy during the wartime.

It was a send-up of much of the wartime legislation and jobsworths issuing pamphlets and guidance aimed to help people, but which really was open to ridicule. It gave birth to characters such as Mrs Mopp and Ali Oop. It spawned catchphrases still in circulation today, such as 'I don't mind if I do', uttered by Colonel Humphrey Chinstrap, used to turn any remark into an offer of a drink, or Mrs Mopp's innuendo-oozing 'Can I do you now sir?' or her sign-off, 'TTFN', standing for 'ta ta for now'. Bunty recalled in her diary:

> We listened to the radio a lot. We especially liked the comedy shows such as ITMA but really we listened to all sorts of things. We made a point of hearing the speeches Winston Churchill was making, the radio was very important to us.

With people staying in more often, businesses were also quick to capitalise on the newly captive audiences with a range of products, from chemistry sets to modelling kits, being distributed to keep people entertained at home. There was even a special blackout card game. War-themed games, such as a dartboard featuring Hitler's head, and a pin the tail on the donkey variation called Decorate Goering, were also sold to help while away the hours of darkness.

Numerous books were also published, subject to paper restrictions (most magazines were still published, but they were half the size of their pre-war selves) offering games, puzzles, quizzes and articles to the bored home-dwellers. One of the most popular was Evelyn August's *The Black-Out Book* which, according to the book's blurb, was 'the ideal companion for those long black-out evenings, with enough entertainment for 101 black-out nights, a book you can safely give as a present to one friend or to an entire family'.

The Blitz began on 7 September 1940 and saw London bombed for fifty-seven nights in a row. The problem London faced was that no matter how dark the streets were kept at night, the River Thames was easily seen by the German bombers, especially in bright moonlight, and could guide them to their targets. (Courtesy of Shutterstock)

Thanks to its factories and docks, London's East End was the first to be targeted by the Luftwaffe and suffered the worst damage in the city. (Courtesy of Shutterstock)

St Paul's Cathedral remained a beacon of hope for Londoners. Despite the odds, and thanks to its highly efficient team of fire-watchers, the cathedral suffered little damage during the bombing raids. (Courtesy of Shutterstock)

Train services were just one of the many aspects of London life disrupted by bomb damage. (Courtesy of Shutterstock)

Being a firefighter was one of the busiest jobs in London during the war, not to mention the many people from other professions who volunteered for the Auxiliary Fire Service. (Courtesy of Shutterstock)

Many volunteered to join Air Raid Precautions (ARP) and as fire-watchers. (Courtesy of Shutterstock)

Bomb damage was extensive in London. (Courtesy of Shutterstock)

Hundreds of thousands of Londoners lost their homes, their only possessions being those that could be salvaged from the rubble. (Courtesy of Shutterstock)

London's streets were strewn with debris, rubble and fire hoses. (Courtesy of Shutterstock)

Thousands of London homes were damaged by bombs and fires.
(Courtesy of Shutterstock)

Though many people chose to shelter from air-raids in the underground stations, they were not necessarily safe. One hundred and eleven people died after a bomb landed on Bank station in January, 1941. (Unknown)

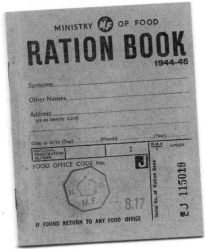

Food rationing began in January 1940, with bacon, ham, butter and sugar. Fresh meats, margarine, preserves and cheese all joined the list in the following year. Everybody was issued with a ration book like this which enabled them to claim their quota.
(Courtesy of Shutterstock)

Plenty of advice was issued to homeowners on what to do in the event of an air-raid. This is one such poster which suggests people are ready to react if raiders visited at night. (Courtesy of Shutterstock)

For the first few months, the most notable change war wrought on Britain was the black-out. Motorists had to make their cars compliant with the regulations, most obviously by masking the headlights, as demonstrated in this picture by Bunty's father Alf and his vehicle.
(Courtesy of the Leatherdale family)

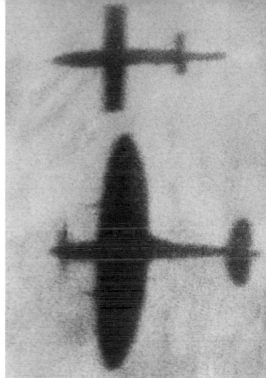

Later in the war the Germans attacked London with V-1 rockets. They were deadly when they hit their target but many either failed to reach London or were destroyed by the city's air defence system. (Courtesy of Shutterstock)

Here a Spitfire flies close to a V-1 rocket bound for London in an attempt to destabilise the pilotless bomb. (Courtesy of Shutterstock)

THE MEALS IN ESTABLISHMENTS ORDER, 1942.

By the terms of this Order, it is not permissible :

(1) to serve or consume more than three courses at a meal.

(2) to serve or consume food after midnight.

(3) to exceed the authorised charges

These are :

HOUSE CHARGE - - - - 6/-
MAXIMUM for FOOD - - - 6/-
      with OYSTERS 8/6
DANCING - - - - - 2/6

SAVOY HOTEL

G. Leatherdale
Elsie G Chalmers.

Donald G. Chalmers

Jas Chalmers.

A Leatherdale.

Dennis Leatherdale

In 1943, Bunty, her parents and some family friends had their Christmas dinner at the Savoy hotel. These two pictures show the menu they had to choose from, as well as the signatures of all those in their party. The Meals in Establishments Order of 1942 restricted the number of courses restaurants could serve and the price they could charge. (Courtesy of the Leatherdale family)

SAVOY RESTAURANT

FROM SEVEN-THIRTY O'CLOCK
Christmas Dinner
ARTHUR SALISBURY and Orchestra

AFTER EIGHT O'CLOCK
Presentation of Christmas Pudding

FROM NINE O'CLOCK
Dancing to
CARROLL GIBBONS and
THE SAVOY HOTEL ORPHEANS
ARTHUR SALISBURY and Orchestra

CHRISTMAS DAY, 1943.

DINER DE NOEL

*

Les Frivolités Savny
la Tasse de Tortue au Sherry

*

La Dinde du Norfolk Farcie aux
Marrons du Dorset
Les Cœurs de Céleris Voilés
au Fromage du Pays
La Fontaine des Florentins
Les Feuilles Citronées Bon Espoir

*

Le Plum Pudding aux Etincelles Joyeuses
La Sauce aux Trois Etoiles Bordelaises
Le Fin Mince Pie
La Bûche de Noël

Thousands descended into the underground network each night to seek shelter from the bombs. Though initially reluctant to allow it, the government realised it could do little to stop the shelter-seekers so took measures to make them more comfortable. At Holborn, bunks were installed for the weary Londoners.
(Courtesy of the Daily Herald Archive/National Media Museum/Science & Society Picture Library)

After the V-1 flying bombs came the V-2 rockets, fearsome when they found their targets. To prevent public terror and the Germans from knowing they had found their aim, the first few V-2 strikes on England were reported as domestic incidents such as gas main explosions.
(Courtesy of the Science Museum/Science & Society Picture Library)

Evelyn August was actually the pen name of the book's compilers, married couple Sydney and Muriel Box. The first issue, which was published in November 1939, sold out within a few months. In recent years it has been reproduced by Osprey publishing.

The book is broken up into activities for each night, featuring puzzles, tests, and humorous and uplifting articles. A cartoon on the fifth night shows a blonde lady going to the hairdresser and asking him to dye her hair black.

'Black madam?' responds the stylist. 'Yes,' says the lady, 'my boy's an ARP warden and he says he can't take me out because I contravene the black-out regulations.'

There were also diagrams and descriptions of puzzles people could do with matchsticks, such as special arrangements or using them to solve mathematical problems. The twelfth night's chapter taught magic tricks, while the seventeenth encouraged readers to come up with silly similes. Numerous chapters contained drawings of the stars and constellations, which had become visible thanks to the blackout.

There were also activities for young people, such as the scouts and various military-cadet programmes. John Sweetland was a member of the Saint Pancras Sea Scouts, which would meet every Sunday aboard the RRS *Discovery*, the ship in which Captain Scott sailed to the Antarctic. The vessel was moored opposite Temple Station. Sweetland was very proud of the fact that his troupe were allocated Captain Scott's cabin for their meetings. The *Discovery* was run by a former sailor and manned by a group of teenage orphans.

Some swimming pools also remained open, subject to blackout conditions, and bomb damage of course. Going for a dip was then, as now, a popular pastime for many young people, although there could also be hazards of a more human nature, as recalled by 14-year-old John Sweetland. Before they were hit by a bomb and closed, Marshall Street swimming baths were Sweetland's waters of choice. However, Sweetland wrote of one attendant who enjoyed engaging in 'blatant exhibitions of homosexual groping', adding:

> The attendant would wait until boys were retrieving their clothes, standing shivering in their clinging wet costumes at the counter, and then make a sudden lunge at their genitals exclaiming 'you've got a big one'.

Just because there was a war on, it did not prevent people having fun.

Chapter Six

Wartime Holidays In and Around the Capital City

Some seventy years before it was even a word, wartime Britons were partaking in the 'staycation'.

Travel abroad was, for obvious reasons, tricky, while moving around the UK was also discouraged to preserve fuel and keep public transport available for those who really needed it, such as servicemen and government officials.

The 'Holiday at Home' campaign was launched in 1942, which, as the name suggests served to encourage people to stay at home for their holidays rather than make unnecessary journeys.

'There are lots of advertisements urging people to "stay put" for their holidays this year', wrote Joan Strange, a diarist from Worthing, in her diary on 4 July 1943. 'There are bands etc in the parks to entice Londoners to stay.'

On 22 August, she noted: 'Crowds everywhere in London – people are having 'stay at home' holidays. We went on the river for two hours; you can't go for less time and you pay a deposit as soldiers have been leaving the boats anywhere.'

For young people in London, there were plenty of entertainments and amusements with which to fill their holiday time, although concessions had to be made because of the war. London Zoo, for example, closed at 11.00 am on the first day of the war, but reopened to the public again just twelve days later. Visitors on 15 September 1939, however, would have seen some changes.

The zoo's most valuable animals were moved thirty-four miles northwest to Whipsnade in Bedfordshire. The 'evacuees' included a pair of giant pandas, three Asian elephants, four chimpanzees, two orangutans and an ostrich. The animals may well have disliked the journey, but they were the lucky ones. All the venomous animals – such as the snakes and spiders – were euthanised with chloroform to avoid their escape in the event of a bomb damaging the zoo.

Numerous fish were also destroyed when the zoo's 165,000-gallon aquarium was emptied, not only to prevent problems if a bomb struck, but also to save on the cost of keeping the tank and its inhabitants going. Although the zoo reopened quickly, the aquarium remained closed until May 1943. According to the Zoological Society of London, the carp ended up in Three Island Pond where the flamingos lived, while the most valuable fish were kept in small tubs and tanks in the Tortoise House, the windows of which having been taped up in that distinctive crisscross pattern to prevent shattering.

Other zoo animals had to work for their living. With petrol rationed, the camels and llamas became the zoo's main methods of transporting food and goods around the various animal houses. The diminutive Shetland ponies were entrusted with short journeys beyond the zoo's walls.

Of course, feeding the animals was a challenge. The pelicans, for example, had to get used to eating meat covered in fish-liver oil as their preferred meal of fish had become prohibitively expensive. Radio appeals were made for acorns to help feed other animals. The British public, well known for being a nation of animal lovers, rallied. The zoo's monkeys, deer, squirrels and rodents were kept well fed with buckets of acorns arriving every week. The zoological society also turned 200 acres of land at Whipsnade into fields for growing wheat and other crops for their herbivores. Money for food was also raised through the zoo's adopt-an-animal scheme, a 'temporary' project that is still going strong today.

The zoo was hit several times by bombs, with damage ranging from broken glass to blown-up buildings. On 27 September 1940, the gardener's office, sheds and houses of the rodents, civets, and zebras were all damaged by several high-explosive bombs. Amazingly, there were no casualties of either human or animal form, but a zebra, and a wild ass and her foal escaped. The zebra was recaptured as it was making its way towards Camden Town. Some humming birds also seized the chance to fly for freedom – they were never recovered. Later that same night, the zoo's main restaurant was set alight when more than thirty firebombs fell. The zoo was also closed for a week because of an unexploded bomb. One other notable incident came in January 1941, when the camel house was hit. Keepers, no doubt fearing the worst for their ships of the desert, were amazed to find the camels happily eating away in the ruins of their former home.

The zoo remained a popular attraction – and possibly a distraction – for many during the war. Although the number of visitors inevitably dropped – 1.6 million people visited in 1943 compared to 2 million before the war – an impressive number still remained, determined to enjoy their trips to see the animals. Members of the armed forces could get in for half price on weekdays and free on Sundays, while the wounded were welcome at all times at no charge.

The capital's museums also tried to carry on, although many of their priciest exhibits were put away for safekeeping. The British Museum, for example, effectively requisitioned Aldwych Tube Station as a repository for one of its main treasures, the Parthenon Sculptures, better known as the Elgin Marbles. The 100-ton stone sculptures were taken in crates by low-loader lorry to the London Transport depot at Lillie Bridge in Kensington, from where they were transferred to the railway to be taken underground. They remained there until 25 November 1948.

With passenger services to the station suspended on 21 September 1940, Aldwych for a few months also became the wartime home to collections from the museum's library, as well as an air-raid haven with capacity for 2,500 shelter seekers.

Joan Strange went to the British Museum on 22 February 1941. 'There is very little left to see as all the most precious things have been stored in safer places', she wrote.

The Victoria and Albert Museum (V&A), another popular tourist attraction, also used Aldwych in which to store its ceramic collection. Other items were initially moved to Montecute House in Somerset, but, amid fears of the stately home's proximity to aircraft factories that could be targeted by bombers, they ended up underground at Westwood Quarry near the Wiltshire town of Bradford-in-Avon. The V&A did close, in September 1939, to sort out its collections in anticipation of the feared bombers, but reopened on 13 November that year. A shelter large enough for 450 people, created in a reinforced basement, was made available for visitors to use during air raids. The pictures from the National Gallery were removed and taken to an old slate quarry in North Wales.

Shortly before war was declared, Kenneth Clark, the director of the gallery, told the BBC in August 1939:

We decided to take the pictures there by rail rather than by road because it really is much smoother and more certain. The only difficulty was that three of our biggest pictures would not go through any tunnels. To meet this difficulty a member of staff who is a mathematician thought of that old idea which used to be such a nuisance to us at school called the theorem of Pythagoras. He constructed a case by which these big pictures were tilted slightly

on their side and the upright part of the case was just low enough
to pass through all the tunnels.

The gallery itself became a temporary concert venue during this period in
its history.

The Natural History Museum, another popular haunt for residents of
and visitors to London was also struck, as noted by photographer Cecil
Beaton, who was tasked by the Ministry of Information to photograph the
aftermath of air raids. He wrote in his diary, extracts of which were published
by Carol Harris in *Blitz Diary*:

> The curator showed me the damage. *The Times* had minimized the
> damage. Why, the herbarium had been burnt out by an incendiary
> bomb, and that was the centre of interest of all the botanists in
> the world. Vitrines by the acre were smashed to smithereens, the
> carcasses of prehistoric animals had gone to dust, and the force of
> an explosion had caused a sheet of writing paper to cut a crack right
> through a mahogany cupboard door.

Madame Tussauds was another popular attraction, as it had been since
it opened in 1835, first on Baker Street then on Marylebone Road.
However, it was devastated during the opening flurries of the Blitz. The
cinema, which had been built in 1928, three years after the attraction was
destroyed by a blaze, was blown apart by a single, high-explosive bomb on
9 September 1940.

Writer Virginia Woolf saw for herself the damage caused to the cinema,
making a note about it in her diary the day after the raid: 'The cinema behind
Madam Tussauds torn open. The stage visible, some decoration swinging.'

More than 350 head molds were also destroyed. Ironically, one of the
heads to survive was that of Adolf Hitler, although his nose was chipped,
according to *Daily Express* reporter Hilde Marchant,

> … and Goering's magnificent white coat was covered with black
> dust. It was a macabre joke, stepping over wax arms and torn wax
> torsos. Naturally I had hoped Hitler was broken, but little had
> happened to that gang. The head boy himself had slipped to one
> side and chipped a lump out of his face. Pleasingly, Churchill stood
> as firm as a rock, his glassy blue eyes sternly supervising the clearing
> of the wreckage.

Despite the damage, the attraction was open again by the end of 1940, although the cinema never returned.

Trips to the seaside have long been a favourite pastime for Londoners, a chance to swap the sooty city air for the bracing salt spray of the swelling and ebbing sea. The towns along the south coast, which had thrived and thronged with visitors in earlier years – consider the Victorians' penchant for Brighton – suddenly became the first line of Britain's land-based defences. These coastal resorts had now become defence areas, meaning visitors would need a permit to be able to enter them. As Angus Calder writes, 'sea-front hotels were requisitioned, machine guns sprouted from piers, bathing was prohibited on many beaches, barbed wire straggled everywhere, curfews were imposed.'

On Wednesday, 24 March 1943, Bunty and her family went for one last jaunt to Brighton before it was closed to visitors. She wrote:

> Today I played truant from the hospital and spent a grand day at Brighton with Mummy, Daddy and Uncle Chris. The ban prohibiting visitors to Brighton begins at the end of this month so we thought we'd get in while the going's good. It was lovely to smell the sea again after two years, even though the defences prevented us seeing much of it. We had a nice enough lunch at the Ship Hotel and spent the afternoon walking almost the entire length of the promenade, then back to the Ship for tea and home about 8.30. It's been a wonderful day.

'My uncle Chris lived in Brighton,' Bunty told me many years later. 'We went to see him once or twice during the war, but for a lot of the time we simply weren't allowed to visit, the whole of the coast was fortified.'

In her diaries, Joan Strange saw her hometown of Worthing, a seaside town on the West Sussex coast some sixty miles south of London, prepare for war. On 6 July 1940, she wrote:

> Driving along Worthing front this morning I noticed how rapidly it had been converted into a battle front. Machine guns hidden under shingle and sand-bags, ammunition dumps disguised as beach chalets and so on. The papers say we are now a 'defence area', which means no one can come here except with official permission. Worthing looks quite empty with no visitors and so many inhabitants moving inland.

John Sweetland recalls a family holiday to Lyme Regis in August 1940 when he was 14 years old:

> Father was an obstinate man, he was determined to take the annual August family holiday as had been the practice before the war. Despite being warned of the foolhardiness of such a venture with an invasion expected at any time, we were to holiday at the worst possible place, on the south coast at Lyme Regis.

As they neared Southampton, however, a group of German planes flew above their coach, causing the driver to park the vehicle next to a large hedge.

> 'I don't think we should go on,' [the driver] said. Those passengers not still cowering in silence, father included, pointed out the choice of being stranded, returning to London or taking the chance of driving on. The choice was made; having come so far we would drive on to Southampton.

They were met with dock fires, craters in the roads and bodies 'now beyond help', covered by sacks and sections of old linoleum, 'their legs stuck stiffly out'. 'This was the real thing', Sweetland wrote, having at this point previously only seen air raids on the newsreels: 'The sight of partly demolished houses, the smoke, dust and smells aroused in me mixed feelings of disbelief and excitement.'

Sweetland and his parents completed their journey by train, but the drama did not end when they reached Lyme Regis. As they were walking to their hostel, they heard gunfire overhead, and watched as a Dornier bomber was hit and crashed in flames into the sea, two of its occupants being seen to parachute to safety.

A few days later, while enjoying a relaxing day on the beach, the peace was again disturbed, this time by a Heinkel HE-III bomber flying low and fast directly towards him:

> As the plane was upon me with a deafening roar, I could plainly see the gunner, prone in the perspex nose, grinning and waving like Royalty. With a very uneasy feeling in my stomach, I thanked everything possible that the gunner hadn't used the machine gun.

The plane was subsequently shot down at the Somerset town of Yeovil. By the time Sweetland returned from his seaside holiday, the Battle of Britain was beginning, and London had already seen its first night of raids.

The seaside towns became the drop-off point for army evacuees from France, most notably those escaping Dunkirk. Pilot Richard Hillary visited Brighton shortly after the evacuation of Dunkirk, which had seen 338,226 Allied soldiers rescued from the French coast by a flotilla of fishing boats, private yachts and military ships, just as they faced capture from the advancing Germans.

'The beaches, streets and pubs were a crawling mass of soldiers, British, French and Belgian', he wrote in his memoirs *The Last Enemy*. 'They had no money but they were being loyally welcomed by the locals. The most frequent request was for somewhere to bathe their feet.'

Some youth groups would organise camping trips during the holidays. In 1942, John Sweetland went on one such excursion with the Sea Scouts to Penton Hook, a campsite on a small island in the middle of the River Thames, near Slough. The trip was momentarily in jeopardy when he and his troop were challenged by an officious member of the Home Guard who, armed with a fixed bayonet, demanded they explain what they were up to, ordering them to show some identification. 'I had heard of parachutists disguised as nuns', Sweetland later wrote, 'but as Sea Scouts, took some believing.'

The rest of their trip involved swimming in the Thames, cooking food and 'jolly old singsongs around the camp fire'.

War? What war?

Chapter Seven

Fashion on the Ration

As with teenagers today, for many wartime youngsters, image was vitally important. Even during a war, people still wanted to impress with their dress. The war just meant that they had to be a bit more creative to achieve the desired look.

On 1 July 1941, clothes joined food in being rationed. This was for two main reasons. Firstly, the material to make clothes from was not arriving in as large a quantity, and a lot of what did come was needed to make military or war-related garments – about a quarter of the population was entitled to or needed some form of uniform.

'There is enough for all if we share and share alike', trumpeted a pamphlet issued by the Board of Trade. 'All honest people realise that trying to beat the ration is the same as trying to cheat the nation', it concluded.

Secondly, the government wanted more of those working in the clothing industry to turn their attentions to manufacturing munitions and other war work. The introduction of clothes' rationing freed up about 450,000 workers, who moved into other more vital production areas.

'Rationing was not just a restriction', wrote Angus Calder, 'it was a promise that a fair and useful share would be available for all.'

People were issued with clothing coupons that they needed to use carefully and wisely in conjunction with cash. In the first year of coupon use, people were allocated sixty-six points each. This dropped to forty in September 1943, then to just twenty-four for the eight months between September 1945 and April 1946.

A new suit for a man would 'cost' twenty-six points, a shirt five, a woollen dress for a woman eleven points, and a pair of stockings two. People still had to pay for their clothes even with the coupons and this could be very expensive. Prices soared in the early years of the war, sometimes tenfold. For example, a nightie, which would have cost the modern day equivalent of £1.25 at the start of the war, would have set a person of the early 1940s back £12. Not all clothes were rationed, although the usefulness of some of these items was questionable. Ballet shoes, belts, clogs and shoelaces all fell under the coupon-free article section of the Board of Trade's *Clothing Coupon Quiz* leaflet. Certain aspects of military uniforms, such as trousers and tunics, were also ration free.

The leaflet also notes that shoppers can buy just one sock, shoe or glove – using half the coupons a full pair would cost – as long as the 'shopkeeper does not object'. In 1942, with forty-eight coupons a year, an average man could, according to Angus Calder, procure:

> One pair of socks every four months, one pair of shoes every eight months, one shirt every twenty months, one vest and one pair of pants every two years, one pair of trousers and one jacket every two years, one waistcoat every five years, one pullover every five years and an overcoat every seven years leaving about three coupons a year for such odd items as handkerchiefs.

To help ease the burden of needing to own the right attire, the Archbishop of Canterbury, William Temple, issued an edict that women who were morally good and without impropriety could attend church without needing to wear hats or stockings.

At the end of 1941, and into the beginning of 1942, the government introduced effectively its own line of clothing: the utility range, branded CC41 – standing for either the Civilian Clothing Order 1941 or Controlled Commodity. The distinctive logo, designed by Reginald Shipp, became known as the 'double cheese', as the two Cs were thickened – picture two Trivial Pursuit wheels with only five instead of six wedges in each. The aim was to reduce the amount of materials being used by the clothing industry, while also producing cheaper clothes for the general public.

To this end, the CC41 range featured items devoid of such frivolities and excesses as turn-ups on trousers, double breasts on suit jackets, pleats in skirts, and a limit on the number of buttons and pockets. Some two inches of material were removed from men's shirttails, while their socks could be no longer than nine-and-a-half inches. Such restrictions were lifted in 1944, much to the improvement of the morale of men who had objected to the loss of their turn-ups and long socks. 'The morale of women has always been high,' remarked Hugh Dalton, who had been appointed president of the Board of Trade in 1942, 'but that of the men has been depressed by not having enough pockets.'

It is estimated that such measures saved about four-million square yards of cotton a year.

Clothes were made from a limited range of quality controlled fabrics, the prices being controlled to prevent profiteering by the manufacturers.

The utility system actually worked quite well for many poorer people, as it guaranteed a particular quality that, previously, was far from certain. In effect, shoppers knew that they were spending their precious coupons and money on items of war that would last, unlike some of the cheaper non-utility clothes.

Made from controlled cloths, featuring new qualities such as a crease resistance and designed by top fashion designers, the CC41 clothes were very popular. It also helped that they were significantly cheaper than the non-utility clothes. A CC41 child's coat, for example, cost two-fifths of a non-CC41 garment. The government could tell manufacturers what to make, and by May 1942, four-fifths of the clothes being made were 'utility'.

Utility schemes were also launched to produce goods such as carpets, lighting, umbrellas, musical instruments, pencils and domestic electrical appliances, all to ensure that the depleted work force could be at its most efficient while also conserving raw materials. Crockery was white. Time-wasting floral patterns were banned, and cups and mugs were made without handles. These were essential measures to meet the shortfall of an anticipated one-hundred million pieces of crockery needed each year. The production of non-essential forms of cutlery, such as grape scissors or asparagus eaters, was also banned, as were most leather goods and all glassware, apart from simple jugs, tumblers or mugs, and small mirrors.

Furniture too was produced under the utility scheme. From August 1942, the production of all but twenty-two types of furniture was banned. Those deemed important enough to still be made, had to contain a certain amount of timber, and typically came in no more than three designs. Angus Calder wrote:

> They were simple and serviceable, and although hardboard was used instead of plywood and a matt finish instead of the usual polishes, the utility pieces at their best made an aesthetic virtue out of austerity.

Furniture was issued under a coupon scheme with priority given to newlyweds setting up a new home and those who had lost their possessions in air raids.

With new clothes difficult to come by, the 'Make Do and Mend' campaign was launched to encourage the country to repair and maintain their existing wearables. Sewing, knitting and darning became key skills and pastimes for many women and men. People also found other materials from which to make their clothes, such as curtains and old blankets. Women would refashion the suits left behind by their war-bound husbands into jackets and skirts. Government pamphlets were released featuring characters such as Mrs Sew-and-Sew, aimed to inspire and educate householders on how to make their clothes last.

One such leaflet, number eight in the Make Do and Mend series issued by the Board of Trade, offered women advice on how to become a 'clothes doctor'. Tips included how to lengthen a dress or tailor a baggy skirt, how to give an old coat a fresh start, or how to keep pace with a growing girl. Another one of Mrs Sew-and Sew's tips was to make slippers for the family from scraps.

'Slippers save a lot of wear and tear on outdoor shoes and can be made quite easily at home', the Board of Trade's leaflet advised, complete with illustrations and diagrams.

Of course, growing children had no choice but to get new clothes. They received extra coupons as the government recognised their need for new attire on a more regular basis. The Women's Voluntary Service set up clothing exchanges, where parents could swap clothes now too small for their offspring in exchange for points to buy new ones. Mothers were also advised to buy larger sizes for their children to grow into.

Stockings were primarily made from silk at the beginning of the war, but this was needed in the war machine to make parachutes. Similarly, nylon, the revolutionary new material developed by American-firm Dupont in 1939 to make fashionable stockings, and which arrived in Britain in the 1940s, was now needed in the manufacture of parachutes and rope.

Women's desire for stockings and indeed society's expectation on them to wear them, however, did not initially diminish, so they had to don their thinking caps. In lieu of stockings, women would paint their legs with tanned creams or liquids, most famously gravy or tea, which was fine so long as it did not rain. They would draw seams up the back of their bare legs with eyeliner pencils. Some entrepreneurial hopefuls even set up shops and booths where, for about a penny a leg, women could have their fake stockings applied for them. Later on in the war, specific make-up for the legs started to be sold. There were also products such as the 'liquid-silk' stockings, which, according to the packaging, gave 'bare legs the elegance of sheer silk'.

Elastic was another commodity for which the supply was stretched. Under the government's austerity measures, only a very small number of clothing items were allowed to be fitted with elastic. Chief among these was women's underwear. It could be embarrassing when a lady's underwear elastic went while out in public, as recalled by Londoner Edith Smith in Anton Rippon's book *How Britain Kept Calm and Carried On: True Stories from the Home Front*:

> You had a couple of options. You could bend down and take them from around your ankles and put them in your handbag, which was humiliating, or you could step out of them and walk on as though nothing had happened, but then you would lose a perfectly good pair of knickers. Actually there was a third option – if you had enough warning. When you felt them going you might be able to grab them from outside your dress, and then do a funny walk until you found somewhere private where you could sort them out. That happened to me once when a boy was taking me to the pictures. I managed to get into the ladies' toilets but I think he'd already spotted that something was wrong from the way I was walking, all bandy-legged all of a sudden. Still, it was wartime, we had to carry on.

Men had to rely on braces and belts to keep their trousers up. Elastic waistbands and zip fasteners were banned.

It wasn't just the people who wanted to make themselves look nice and presentable. The government too was encouraging people not to let their styles and standards drop, fearing that people who gave up on their appearance may also be giving up on the war. In short, women needed make-up for the nation's morale. Some cosmetics companies dropped their make-up manufacturing so they could produce other chemicals and powders to fuel the war machine. So, though make-up was never actually rationed, it did become harder to find and became rather expensive. The ever-resourceful ladies, however, were not to be beaten and they found workarounds. For example, boot polish masqueraded as mascara, beetroot juice made a decent deputy for lipstick, and rose petals soaked in red wine were used as rouge. The remains of old lipsticks would be scooped out and melted down to form a new bar. Charcoal, soot, or boot polish could act as eyeliner, while lard substituted for make-up remover.

In his book of 1940, *They Can't Ration These*, the Vicomte de Mauduit offers several natural solutions for cosmetics shortages. Marshmallow root boiled, cooled, and then mixed with honey, would provide a lotion to produce a 'fresh complexion'. Elderflowers boiled in water or horseradish mixed with sour milk could cover freckles. De Mauduit also notes that rubbing one's teeth with sage twice a day, and washing them after every meal with tepid water and a few drops of myrrh, would 'prevent the teeth from discolouring and decaying'.

Obviously, the public were encouraged to make what little they had last. In her diary, Bunty notes how she goes longer between hair washings. Jayne Shrimpton in *Fashion in the 1940s*, wrote:

> A clear complexion, bright lips and accentuated eyes, along with a feminine hairstyle and jewellery, could almost compensate for old, uninspiring clothes and down-at-heel shoes. Beauty products and the many substitutes used during the years of austerity played an important role, helping women to maintain the impression of a normal appearance and, especially, enhancing their sense of femininity and self-esteem.

Such was the importance of fashion to morale, Queen Elizabeth made a point of not wearing dark clothes when touring areas of bomb damage.

'Inspired by the semi-mourning colour lilac, she chose muted pastel shades suggestive of hope', wrote Ms Shrimpton.

The Royal family also complied with clothing restrictions. Older outfits were re-used and the Queen's clothes adjusted to fit her daughters, the princesses Elizabeth and Margaret. Propaganda photographs showing glamorous-looking models wearing fashionable steel hats were also released in a bid to encourage women to keep safe while still staying stylish.

Even working long hours in a factory, manufacturing munitions for the war effort, was no excuse. Women were still encouraged to wear make-up, partly because it was believed certain creams would protect the skin from toxic chemicals. In 1942, such workers were awarded a special allowance for face creams. Make-up sales people were reported to have visited factories to physically take their products to the consumers.

People were also encouraged to save water. Even King George VI made a point of never filling his bathtub with more than five inches of water, the government's guideline. The Ministry of Fuel and Power drew up a small poster, with the help of the Hotels and Restaurants Association of Great Britain, to remind customers of the need to save water.

The notice, which was displayed in hotels around the country, said: 'As part of your personal share in the Battle for Fuel, you are asked not to exceed five inches of water in the bath. Make it a point of honour not to fill the bath above this level and also to avoid wastage of water generally.'

Many people painted a black line around their tubs to mark the five-inch depth. Householders were urged to economise on their usage of hot water.

'Did you know it takes about one quarter of all the fuel used in the average home to make cold water hot?' asked a Save Fuel information leaflet.

The government urged citizens to 'use as little hot water as possible' and, when using hot water, ensure it is 'no hotter than necessary'. Households were also asked to only do one wash a week rather than the usual three or four, although the leaflet writers did concede that frequent small washes were 'unavoidable' when dealing with 'baby things'.

On 9 February 1942, soap became the latest commodity to be rationed. This was to allow edible fats to be the priority import rather than the oils and fats used in soap production. Writing in *Spuds, Spam and Eating for Victory*, Katherine Knight said:

> The Minister of Food had a hard choice, he had to decide on behalf of the people if it would be better for them to be clean or well. I can remember the taste of wartime margarine, and on second thoughts, wonder if there was all that much difference between margarine and soap.

For Bunty, as for many Londoners, cleanliness was next to happiness.

On Tuesday, 2 February 1943 – her 18th birthday – she wrote: 'I decided to wash my hair knowing how the result adds greatly to the feeling of looking my best and consequent enjoyment.'

As with previous ration impositions such as the clothing coupons, the soap restriction was implemented swiftly and without warning, to prevent people stockpiling before the rules came into effect. Each person was granted one coupon for soap a week, which equated to about four ounces of regular soap, three ounces of toilet soap, between six and twelve ounces of soap powder, and six ounces of soft soap. Other soaps such as shampoo powder or shaving soap were not rationed at all. Miners were given free soap to use at the colliery baths at the end of their shifts.

From April, mothers were allowed an extra coupon to buy soap for washing baby clothes, as long as their child was under the age of one. Chimney sweeps also received extra in 1945. Therefore, while they did their best to remain looking chic and smart, people may have been a tad smellier than before the war. Forget a shortage of soap, a young lothario might well find his teenage girlfriend smelling of red wine and rose petals, and tasting of beetroot.

Chapter Eight

Making a Meal of Things

Feeding the people was a huge priority for the wartime government. Just because there was a war on, though, it did not mean that Britons no longer expected to be able to go out for dinner. In fact, between 1940 and 1945, the people of Britain ate out more than they ever had before. On average, each citizen would eat four meals a week away from home. For older teenagers, of course, going out meant a time for socialising with friends, and evenings of fun and merriment – air raids permitting. There was also another reason to go out: the food could be considerably better than what was on offer at home. To fully understand the appeal of dining out, first we must understand what they got from staying in. This was dictated by one word – rationing.

Britain's problem was simple to understand. It produced less than a third of the food it needed so relied massively on imports. About ninety per cent of fats and cereals, almost eighty per cent of fruit, some seventy per cent of sugar and cheese, and around fifty per cent of meat was imported. One of Germany's first actions in the war was to target the sea convoys that delivered supplies to Britain. Winston Churchill, who had succeeded Neville Chamberlain as prime minister on 10 May 1940, called it the Battle of the Atlantic.

German submarines – the U-boats – and *Kriegsmarine* warships, supported by the Luftwaffe, blockaded the shipping routes between Europe and the USA. During the six-year struggle, 3,500 merchant vessels and 175 Allied warships, deployed to protect them, were lost, compared to about 780 U-boats.

By 1942, less than half of the pre-war imports were getting into Britain, but once Japan had mounted invasions in the Far East, products such as tea, sugar and rice became much trickier to get, as well as raw materials like tin and rubber. So, with much of their food ending up blown to smithereens or sunk to the bottom of the sea, the British needed to start rationing to ensure everyone had enough to survive.

'The scheme was designed to share out food as fairly as possible', wrote Katherine Knight in *Spuds, Spam and Eating for Victory*.

'Rationing also rammed home the point that the country was at war, giving the nation an all-in-it-together attitude (for most people anyway),' said historian Juliet Gardiner.

Bacon, ham, butter and sugar were rationed in January 1940, followed by fresh meat in March and margarine in July. Preserves joined the ration list in March 1941, with cheese added two months later.

To obtain their allocation, people were issued with ration books – fifty million were printed at the start of the war – that had to be registered with their nearest shop where they had to go to get their groceries. A typical weekly ration in the summer of 1941 for one adult would consist of one pound of meat, eight ounces of sugar, four ounces of bacon, four ounces of margarine, and two ounces each of cheese, tea, butter and cooking fat. Vegetarians were catered for too, being allowed extra cheese in lieu of their unwanted meat.

In July 1942, confectionary was added to the ration list, with people limited to three ounces per person per week. The ingredients of some sweets also changed as milk chocolate became increasingly scarce. KitKat Chocolate Crisp (released by Rowntree in 1935), for example, changed their usual red wrapping to blue to indicate the fact that they were being made from plain chocolate. 'Our standard chocolate crisp will be reintroduced as soon as milk is available', declared a note on the packaging. KitKats reverted to red in 1947.

The packaging of many other products also changed, to what came to be known as their 'wartime jackets'. The new packaging was made from a cheaper cardboard, carrying only the product name. This allowed for the better quality paper to go to the war effort, while also saving on printing ink. 'Temporary wartime packing, contents remained unchanged', was the common slogan on many products, such as Smith's potato crisps, Mazawattee Tea and Orlox plain suet pudding.

In December 1941, a second system was set up to control other foods such as canned goods. This included meats, beans, vegetables and fish, and eventually rice, dried fruits, cereals and biscuits. This was the 'points plan', where people were allocated a certain number of points that they could spend as they liked on the above foods. For example, a can of spam would cost a month's worth of points. A third distribution-plan scheme controlled goods such as milk, both liquid and condensed, as well as eggs, both fresh and dried. People had to register for such commodities, which were handed out when available, with priority being given to certain groups, such as expectant mothers or young children.

It all sounds rather complicated because it was. People could get into trouble for making mistakes with their rations. It was illegal to buy or sell more than the permitted amount of rations.

According to Katherine Knight, it worked, because 'it was perceived to be fair to everyone, which was good for morale at all levels of society. There was enough flexibility to allow for preferences, keeping people comparatively cheerful'.

The rules were strict for sellers of goods, with prices tightly controlled by the government. One notice sent to shoppers and businesses read: 'Shopkeepers who have increased prices are gross and flagrant profiteers. They are charging extra on old stock for old prices therefore robbing the public who are already burdened.'

Wherever government controls exist, one can be almost certain to find people bending or ignoring the rules. This was the black market, where people would buy and sell goods, which they were not supposed to have, at prices not controlled by the government.

In the summer of 1941, Food Minister Lord Woolton claimed there had been 22,356 convictions for rationing and price-control offences since the war had started two years previously. Punishments were tough, with fines often set at three times the value of the goods that had been sold on the black market. Fines of up to £500, or several years in prison, would await anyone caught stealing goods from docks, warehouses or the government's own reserves, which had been created in the event of a German invasion. In total, according to Norman Ferguson in *The Second World War: A Miscellany*, there were 114,000 wartime prosecutions for black-market crimes.

As well as targeting the organised criminals, the government also kept a close eye on shopkeepers. Secret shoppers were often sent to try to negotiate more rations than they were entitled to, often using some form of sob story. Katherine Knight says there was much ill-feeling among shopkeepers against the authorities due to 'petty prosecutions' conducted by the latter.

The food market was open to abuse. Some entrepreneurial ne'er-do-wells created canned substitutes for hard-to-come-by foodstuffs, which were in fact useless. For example, one 'milk' substitute being sold for five shillings a pound merely contained a mixture of flour, salt and baking powder, while onion substitute was simply onion-scented water.

Bread was not rationed until after the war, but it was tightly controlled with the introduction of the National Loaf. This was bread made of eighty-five per cent wholemeal flour with added vitamins and calcium. It was churlishly nicknamed, by some, as 'Hitler's secret weapon'. It is fair to say that it was not that well liked, as it was quite dense and heavy. Even the royal family ate it. It was served to Eleanor Roosevelt, wife of American President Franklin D. Roosevelt, during her visit to Buckingham Palace in 1942.

In *The Queen's House: A Social History of Buckingham Palace*, Edna Healey reports the First Lady saying: 'We were served on gold and silver plates, but our bread was the same kind of war bread every other family had to eat.'

Being a baker's daughter meant Bunty would rarely have experienced a shortage of the National Loaf, but she said she also doesn't really remember being without much of any food:

> Being bakers we weren't quite as short of food, we got preferential treatment for ingredients as what we were producing was so important to people. In fact the bakery business was a very important commodity. In the First World War it was a reserved occupation (just as it would be again in the second) so my father didn't have to join up. He did though because he was patriotic, his older brother Chris and my mother ran it for him while he was away.

Being a baking family also meant the Leatherdales could work closely with other food producers. Bunty recalls:

> I don't remember ever being hungry during the war. My father had a lot of friends and he was a Rotarian and a Mason and they were all in different sorts of businesses, arrangements and agreements could be made between them.

Vegetables were not rationed, but people were encouraged to 'dig for victory' and grow as much of their own as they could. Around 6,000 allotments were opened in London's parks as part of the 30,000 plots in the London area.

The palaces also had to play their part. Gardens at Kensington Palace, for example, were used for cabbage cultivation, while Brussels sprouts were grown at Buckingham Palace, which was hit by a bomb in 1943. Top soil was laid on the filled-in Regent's Canal Basin to provide allotments. By 1943, there were an estimated 1.4 million allotments across the country, each producing about seven pounds of vegetables a week. By that time, it was also calculated that allotments were growing about ten per cent of all food produced in Britain. Many even took to growing vegetables in the eighteen-inch-deep soil used to cover the tops of their Anderson shelters.

Potatoes and root vegetables replaced meat at the core of most meals. Scientific studies were carried out to identify ways to optimise the ration, and it was found potatoes, in particular, were an important part of keeping people going (to be precise, carbohydrates were key, and potatoes were the most available source).

Characters such as Dr Carrot and Potato Pete – who had his own song, performed by Betty Driver, later to find fame in Coronation Street – were created to encourage people to grow them. Potato Pete also had his own series of nursery rhymes, such as 'Jack Sprat could eat no fat, his wife could eat no lean, so they both ate potatoes and scraped their platters clean'.

The claim that carrots could help you see in the dark also originated at this time. Designed to get people to eat more, it also offered an explanation to the Germans as to why RAF pilots were having such success in nighttime duels and raids. The RAF did not want the enemy to know that they had actually developed a very effective radar system.

Both the Ministry of Food and the Ministry of Agriculture released posters urging householders to grow their own vegetables. Farmers were giving most of their land over to the production of essentials such as potatoes, barley, wheat and feed for dairy animals. One poster, aimed at women, declared:

> Farmers are growing more of the essential crops, it's up to you to provide the vegetables that are vital to your children's health – especially in winter. Grow all you can. If you don't, they may go short. Turn your garden over to vegetables.

One organisation that really pushed its members to take up gardening was the Women's Institute, although some of them still recognised the worth of keeping some flowers instead of turning the whole lot over to vegetables and other edibles. In a WI newsletter reproduced by Julie Summers in *Jambusters*, one branch chairwoman advised members not to rip up every flower bed.

'Many beds, such as narrow front gardens, are not suitable for vegetables and we shall always need flowers to bring relief from the nervous strain and stress of wartime life', she wrote.

One of the most famous wartime meals was the Woolton Pie, named after Lord Woolton, minister for food in the imaginatively named Ministry of Food, which had been created at the start of the war to help people cope with their eating requirements.

Millions tuned into the BBC Home Service at 8.15 am every morning to hear a broadcast from the Ministry of Food, offering guidance and tips for food conservation and meal creation. The Woolton Pie epitomised the importance of the vegetables. Mainly made of root vegetables, with a potato and oatmeal pastry, the pie was often served with oatmeal sauce and raw cabbage salad. Lunch would consist of potato or lettuce and margarine sandwiches, made using the National Loaf. Though they were eating less meat and dairy products, many people actually felt the benefit of a better diet as they were consuming more vegetables. By 1944, the average person's calorie intake had risen to about 3,010 a day.

People also had to become creative in their kitchens. About ninety per cent of the nation's cereal was imported, so once the war started, favourite foodstuffs like shredded wheat became a rarity. Wheaties, which were cubes of stale bread heated in the oven, became their substitute. Bread was also used in the wartime sausage, which, because it consisted of so little actual meat, was not rationed. Some estimates say there was as little as three per cent meat in a wartime sausage. The chief ingredients were gristle and bread.

Recipes for rook and squirrel pies were published in *The Times*, while scientists even investigated the possibility of feeding people plankton. Though high in protein, it was concluded that harvesting the sea-dwelling organisms would be too tricky.

Some did make unusual food work, as in the case of J.R.B. Branson from South Clapham who, in early May 1940, wrote this to a local newspaper:

> I hope that you will spare me space to say, as an advocate for the consumption of grass mowings, that I have eaten them regularly for over three years and off many lawns. The sample I am eating at present comes off a golf green in Mitcham Common.

It may sound as if Mr Branson was playing a practical joke, but British Pathé News even made a short film about the sixty-eight-year-old retired solicitor, which further explained his taste for lawn trimmings. In the clip, he is shown running through the park and leaping over a fence to highlight his athleticism. He also claims he can cycle one-hundred miles a day without feeling tired. He puts the secret to this success all down to his diet.

'Grass,' the film's narrator says, 'contains all the essentials for sufficient nutrition [according to] this exuberant liver.'

Mr Branson said he preferred the freshly cut short cuttings from bowling greens, although 'grass from any lawn' will do. The key 'energising and rejuvenating' element is the chlorophyll, he said. Once he had collected his cuttings, he then thoroughly washed and dried the grass before mixing it into recipes to make it 'more palatable'. One of his favoured dishes consisted of six tablespoons of dried grass, two tablespoons of mangle wurzels, three teaspoons of currants, one tablespoon of uncooked rolled oats and, 'ration card permitting', some sugar. His diet cost him about two shillings a week, which, according to the narrator, is what Mr Branson would call a 'real meal'.

An American study at about the same time claimed that twelve pounds of grass contained more vitamins – with the exception of Vitamin D – than 340 pounds of vegetables and fruit. The consumption of grass as a vegetable, however, never really caught on. Katherine Knight, in *Spuds, Spam and Eating for Victory: Rationing in the Second World War*, writes that it was something the Ministry of Food never really looked at promoting, perhaps because eating grass could be thought of as the 'ultimate desperate fallback and sign of madness, so perhaps they dared not suggest it'.

However, the Ministry of Food certainly did issue plenty of guidance to help people make their food go a little further. One of their key battles was with wastage, a lesson that became lasting, as, to this day, Bunty frowns upon either food or materials being thrown away. Wastage of food also became a criminal offence in August 1940, punishable by up to two years in prison.

Waste was also a moral outrage, as mariners had risked their lives to get those goods into the country in the first place. 'Waste means lives', declared a booklet given to American soldiers being deployed to Britain, to advise them on how best to ingratiate themselves with their hosts:

> Most British food is imported even in peacetimes and for the last two years the British have been taught not to waste the things that their ships bring in from abroad. British seamen die getting these convoys through. The British have been taught this so thoroughly that they now know that gasoline and food represent the lives of merchant sailors. And when you burn gasoline needlessly it will seem to them as if you are wasting the blood of those seamen – when you destroy or waste food you have wasted the life of another sailor.

In 1940, French pilot-turned-author George de Mauduit, better known as the Vicomte de Mauduit, wrote *They Can't Ration These*, a 165-page cookbook utilising other unusual ingredients. In his foreword to the book, David Lloyd-George, who had been the country's prime minister for the second half of the First World War, called de Mauduit's ideas a 'valuable contribution towards our national defence'.

The book included recipes for various nettle meals, from soup to toast, dandelion dishes and cardoon (artichoke thistle) creations. He also makes numerous suggestions for meaty meals using creatures such as hedgehogs, snails and squirrels.

'The hedgehog', he wrote, 'is a delicacy which few people have tasted, perhaps because the uninitiated first think of the prickles'. De Mauduit also recommends numerous recipes for birds.

'Sparrows', he opined, 'are far from despicable', when roasted in the right way. He also offers numerous tips on using substitutes when the preferred ingredients are unavailable. The inner bark of an elm tree could replace some cereals. Flowers and fruits could take the place of oriental-grown teas, and dandelion roots and asparagus plants could make a perfectly passable, if not delicious, coffee. There are even recipes for various fruit- and plant-based wines and beers, as well as medicines, such as limewater in milk to combat hay fever.

So, with all this going on at home, it is perhaps understandable why so many opted to eat out – if they could afford it of course. While food at home was rationed, in the restaurants and hotels it was a different story. There were several options for Londoners fancying a meal out.

First, there were the regular bars, restaurants and hotels. Bunty and her family were regular visitors at several establishments in central London such as the Trocadero and Casa Pepes.

Food was allocated to restaurants, with dishes classed as either 'main', which had more protein (i.e. meat or fish) or 'subsidiary', which had less. Diners were allowed one of each with each meal, although they could swap their main for a second subsidiary. Meals were capped at three courses. This was to stop the wealthy being able to pay for more food, although, as Katherine Knight points out, there was nothing to stop someone visiting several restaurants in one night. People staying at boarding houses or hotels would have to surrender their ration books if they were there for more than five days.

During the war, a second option opened up – the British Restaurant. The main aim of the British Restaurants, or 'BR' as Bunty refers to them in her diary, was to offer food and meals for people bombed out of their homes. However, because they could offer hot dishes for a reasonable price, subsidised by the government, many people just went to them for meals out.

'They were clean and spartan,' notes Jill Norman in her foreword to *Eating for Victory*. 'They were more like works' canteens than restaurants but they provided a nutritious meal,' she said.

In May 1941, approximately 79 million midday meals a week were being eaten in subsidised restaurants, canteens and school dining rooms. This had more than doubled to 170 million by the end of 1944. Typical three-course menus would include dishes like 'skilly', a grated carrot or parsnip with onions, garlic and oatmeal soup, followed by cottage pie with carrots and swede, and finishing with apple crumble. Due to the state subsidy, a three-course meal cost a maximum of about £1.50 in today's money.

The cooking was done by volunteers. London County Council ran about 250 across the city. At their peak, people in the heavily bombed East End had no farther than half a mile to travel to find a British Restaurant. Halls, schools and council buildings all had restaurants opened in them, as well as some more notable buildings such as the Victoria and Albert Museum, Fishmonger's Company and the Royal Veterinary College. One British Restaurant, opposite the entrance to Guy's Hospital, was regularly frequented by Bunty and her friends:

> It just seemed like an ordinary little restaurant although some days the food was better than others. I did find however that eating a big three-course lunch made me not to want work very hard in the afternoons.

Cinemas with restaurants also noticed a huge rise in demand.

According to Guy Morgan in *Red Roses Every Night*, before the war twelve Granada restaurants attached to theatres served 250,000 meals a year, employing three chefs and seventy-five other staff. During the rationing years, nine restaurants served 1.5 million meals a year and employed sixteen chefs and two-hundred staff.

After the evacuation of Dunkirk between 27 May and 4 June 1940, several Granada restaurants were used to feed the refugees. Finding food was a challenge, but one enterprising catering manager for the cinema group turned to Scotland for supplies. Meals made from haggis, gulls' eggs, rooks, salmon, lobsters, crabs and even eagle were served as a result.

But it was not just food that posed a sourcing problem for the cinema restaurants. With crockery and cutlery rationed or hard to come by, many patrons took to stealing these from cinemas. At one point, the Granada restaurants were losing 20,000 pieces of crockery a year. In one year alone, writes Morgan, 2,500 items of cutlery were pilfered. Restaurants resorted to fashioning tablecloths out of bed sheets and dustsheets, while waitresses were dressed in old cotton flour bags.

The good-old English pub also kept going during the war, many becoming places of sanctuary for entire families. American journalist Quentin Reynolds was one of many who sought shelter in a pub during an air raid. He wrote in *The Wounded Don't Cry*: 'The basement had been converted into a shelter. At one end perhaps twenty people slept soundly. I went to the other end where a bar had been improvised. Three men were playing darts.'

Reynolds joined the men in a darts match. 'At least you can't hear the blasted Jerry,' one of the men said cheerily. 'My old woman and the kids have been asleep down the other end for two hours.'

'We sleep here every night,' another man told Reynolds, 'Living underground like bloody moles, but it ain't bad.'

Beer was never rationed, but its strength was reduced by about fifteen per cent due to ingredients such as barley becoming scarcer. The importation of wine from Europe had all but stopped, so some turned to making their own. Gin and brandy also became scarcer, but Scottish-brewed whisky was still available, although much of it was saved to swap with America for arms and food. Whisky was also a popular commodity on the black market, where it would fetch a decent price. So even during the darkest days, Londoners could still enjoy a dram or a pint.

Chapter Nine

Getting From A to B

There might have been a war on, but people still needed to be able to get about, whether it was to go to and from work, attend volunteer rallies and meetings, or simply to meet with friends in the city centre. Before 1939, the private car had risen significantly in popularity, but the war saw many return to public transport. There were more than 2,000,000 cars and over 400,000 motorbikes registered for private use in Britain in 1939. With petrol rationed, and only served upon proof of need, many decided to park up their vehicles for the duration. By 1943, only 718,000 cars and 124,000 motorcycles remained registered as being in use.

So people turned to the trains and buses to get about. The number using trains rose by seventy percent during the war. In any case, then as now, getting around London was easiest done on public transport, the principal forms of which were buses, trains, trolley-buses and the underground, which at that time consisted of eight lines. The bombing raids of the Blitz did much to disrupt the transport routes, but the services were already reduced thanks to rationing. London Transport saw their fuel allocation cut by a quarter, necessitating the withdrawal of some 800 buses from service. Other vehicles were requisitioned for the emergency and military services, although buses from elsewhere in the country boosted the fleet, for example, 400 were sent down from Scotland.

To compensate for the reduction in fuel, some buses were converted to run on gas, but Londoners had to wait for a while before they could rely on them to get around the city. There were a few taxis too but many were repainted grey and used by the Auxiliary Fire Service. In some cases, to ease the struggles of their employees having to travel, councils and companies introduced much longer shifts. For example, thirty-six hour shifts, meaning the staff could reduce the number of journeys they would have to make. They would simply sleep at work.

But even where buses were running, just catching one in the blackout could be a challenge. John Sweetland, a teenager living in London during the war, wrote in his memoirs:

When one eventually found the bus stop, would a bus come? And if it did it was hard to identify. Just two small lights through the louvred blackout masks. And then the driver had to see you. Father's effective way was to shine his dim torch into the road and rotate it vigorously.

Then came the problem of how would we know when to get off. Sometimes the conductor would shout the location of the next stop. Although it was pitch black outside, it was a natural reaction to try and pull aside the edge of the diamond cut into the centre of the green netting stuck over the glass window, but the clear area of the diamond was smeary and messy from glue and many fingers, so this action was a bit pointless. On a well-known route one could judge the whereabouts, mentally following the right and left turns and estimating the straight bits until finally ringing the bell to find that it was the wrong bus stop, resulting in an unpleasant and possibly dangerous walk.

In the *Mass Observation* diaries published by Simon Garfield in *We Are at War*, a young woman living in London, whom Garfield called Eileen Potter, also recalled difficulties in getting trams to stop in the blackout. Like Sweetland's father, her best method to halt the 'dim, ghostly shape rattling along the Kennington Road' was to wave her torch at it.

On another occasion, Sweetland and his parents were trying to get across London the day after a raid, which had seen their street cordoned off due to landmines being dropped in the area. He writes:

> The bus became caught up in a mass of diverted and jammed traffic, which seemed to me to be travelling around in one great circle as the main roads were made difficult by rubble and civil defence vehicles.
>
> Farther on, at the junction of Mile End Road and Cambridge Heath Road, the bus could travel no further forcing us to walk towards Bow, or more truthfully to stumble over rubble, much glass and straggling hoses until we found any bus, which would take us further, with all the while the smell of smoke, damp plaster and bricks, accompanied by the sound of spades on brick as the buried were searched for and pathways cleared through the rubble.

Eventually, they found another coach, which, slowly but surely, rumbling over hoses and navigating around piles of bricks and timber, took them to their destination. Sweetland continues:

It was a tribute to London Transport that anything at all was running. Travel by public transport wasn't easy but accepted. As often as not a bus didn't arrive for ages, and then there were the diversions. I remember alighting on the platform of a central London underground station with very little space between the train doors and the shelterers [sic] spread out with their bedding for the night. The stench was awful.

Trams were also affected by bombs damaging the lines. Even if roads were clear of debris, the surfaces could still be greasy from spilled oil or other chemicals, and slippery when wet from the rain. Many roads included wooden bricks, a throw-back to the Victoria era, which also became slippery. Sweetland describes such experiences:

On more than one occasion a bus skidded dangerously around the corner, the rear end at ninety degrees to the pavement. One time, the front of a bus crashed through the railings of Kinnaird House [where Sweetland worked after finishing school] hitting the front wall leaving the bus front wheels dangling over the area.

By 1944, London was filling up again with buses as other companies from around the country sent their vehicles to the capital. 'It was strange to see a strange-coloured bus turn up from up north or somewhere', Sweetland added.

Heavy raids would often, quite understandably, result in major disruption. For example, on 15 October 1940, all rail services in and out of London were shut off after 410 raiders dropped 538 tons of high-explosive bombs on the city. Several train lines were blocked for months at a time, so London Transport had to appeal for buses from all over the country to be sent to the capital to help keep the commute moving. As Angus Calder notes: 'Black, white, brown, green and blue buses from places as far away as Exeter and Inverness joined the familiar red double-deckers in the streets.'

Boat services were started along the Thames to cover the loss of trams and trolleybus services caused by damage to the overhead lines and the tracks they relied on. Queues one-hundred yards long were the norm at bus stops, and even if punters did manage to board a bus, there was no guarantee, thanks to diversions, that they would end up where they wanted to be.

Trains and rail tracks suffered extensive damage from bombs. Replacing carriages was far from simple, however, as many of the factories producing them before the war were now assigned to making munitions. The cost of travelling by train trebled, while the congestion on board also soared. Reservations were no longer available, and it may be impossible to find a space.

'If trains were not cancelled they were likely to be late', wrote Angus Calder.

One young man, writing for the *Mass Observation* report, documented a journey on the Central Line in November 1940. Each carriage was crowded with more people joining at Chancery Lane. Some said they had been waiting for hours, or had been unable to get on the previous fourteen trains due to the number of people already on board.

The man alighted at Liverpool Street Station to change onto an overland service. The escalator, he noted, was a crush of people. One girl was trying to get down while the crowd was going up. Her cries that she wanted to get past did not go down well with the commuters, so she had no choice but to turn and be carried along by the mass. Apparently some rather rude comments were made.

The trolleybuses, which were electric vehicles powered via overhead lines and were installed in 1931, were particularly susceptible to disruption. At its peak, there were some 60 trolleybus routes across the capital, operating more than 1,100 buses. In a letter written to his brother Will, a teacher from Leytonstone pointed out the main problem in a letter published in *Blitz Diary*:

> This bombing has shown the disadvantages of trolley buses compared with buses. Once the trolleybus route has been hit, the route is blocked as trolleybuses can't go round sideways. Nearly all the mainline termini are closed and many suburban stations.

The London underground, the world's first subterranean railway when it opened in 1863, operated throughout the war, but even when the trains were stopped, the platforms of the tube network were still much in demand. The stations became shelters, with people filing in and taking up their positions on the platform long before the trains actually stopped running for the night at ten o'clock.

American journalist Quentin Reynolds encountered many tube-dwellers on his journeys across London.

'At each station it was always the same', he wrote in *The Wounded Don't Cry*. 'These people were adapting themselves to a new way of life. Many of the women wore heavy slacks, stores now advertise 'shelter slacks' or 'siren suits'.

At Hampstead, Reynolds came across:

> Lots of fairly well-to-do people, though tonight these families were sleeping on the concrete of the tube platforms and stairs. It was difficult to get off the train. Before I could step on the platform, a woman had to move her sleeping child. I picked my way over a thousand sleeping forms before getting to the stairs.

He spoke to several of the families seeking sanctuary on the underground. 'You get used to it,' the woman said. 'Of course the air is bad but at least we know we are safe.'

The tube stations, however, were a far cry from the comforts found at home:

> The night wore on. It grew cold and sometimes people stirred uneasily. Some still read newspapers in the dim light. Those who had tea shared it with those who hadn't. Two policemen were on watch. They kept walking up and down the crowd. Their chief concern was to see that restless children didn't roll off the platform on to the line.

Reynolds struck up a conversation with the officers, asking them what time they would ask those seeking shelter to leave.

'Turn them out?' the policeman asked Reynolds, 'I'd like to see anyone try to turn them out. They usually leave when the all-clear sounds.'

Later on that night, Reynolds found himself at Piccadilly tube station, which, according to a policeman on duty there, was sheltering some 3,000 people that night.

'There was no air-conditioning here, no nurses, no hot canteen', he wrote, comparing the station to the Savoy Hotel, which he had also visited that night and where he had seen a permanent doctor available – 'comfortable cots' and 'always a drink within reach'. The platform and the stairs were jammed with what in the dim light looked to be shapeless untidy bundles', the journalist described the scene, witnessing something not seen for thousands of years. He had seen 'a city asleep in the caves under the ground, modern caves to be sure, but caves none the less'.

'It hadn't been a pleasant night', he concluded.

Britain's road networks and vehicles also had to be prepared for a German invasion. It was feared that, once the Germans set foot on British soil, they would steal any vehicle they could find in order to strengthen their attack. It was decided to make not only getting a vehicle difficult, but also to find their way around the country much more arduous. Buses were fitted with wheel-locking devices when they were off duty, while all private cars were required by law to be immobilized in some way when left for long periods, such as overnight. This usually meant removing the rotor arm from the distributor, but if this had not been done the police would pull out ignition leads or deflate tyres.

There were suddenly fewer petrol pumps in the south and east coastal areas, the spots most vulnerable and likely to be attacked. Plans had been put in place to destroy them all if the invaders made it on to English soil. Other defence measures included large metal poles and girders laid in fields to deter enemy gliders from landing, and big concrete anti-tank blocks positioned on the coastal roads. Signs and street names were also removed. Milestones and war memorials were altered so as to not give any clue as to the location where they were sited. This quickly proved to be confusing, however, so some signs were returned, although their directions were kept so vague as to be almost useless.

Buses and trains also had to contend with far fewer indications of where they might actually be. Station and bus stop name-signs were removed within twenty miles of the coast. In other places, the lettering was no more than three-inches high. In a letter to the weekly review *Time and Tide*, novelist George Orwell had even suggested that these measures did not go far enough:

> Painting out place names, this has been well done as regards signposts, but there are everywhere shopfronts, tradesmen's vans, etc, bearing the name of their locality. Local authorities should have the power to enforce the painting out of these immediately. This should include the brewers' names on public houses. Most of these are confined to a fairly small area and the Germans are probably methodical enough to know this.

In the blackout, of course, there was little way of seeing exactly where one was, and there were numerous accounts of passengers missing their stops and stations. So getting from A to B in London was certainly possible – hundreds of thousands of people still did it on a daily basis. They just had to accept that, sometimes, they might actually end up going via C, or could finish their journey at D.

Chapter Ten

Censorship and Sensitivity

In a time of war, information is a powerful weapon. It can spread panic and fear and demoralise a population to the point of mutiny. Alternatively, it could provide pivotal knowledge to the enemy, giving him the code for unlocking the door of defence. To prevent these things from happening, news and public messages in Britain were controlled. Such information was issued by the Ministry of Information, a government department first set up towards the end of the First World War, and resurrected for the latest one. By 1943, the ministry had 2,900 employees, including 200 journalists.

There were three principal aims for the ministry. Firstly, the censoring of newspapers, newsreels and radio broadcasts. Secondly, producing information for the Home Front, and thirdly, creating publicity for other nations, mainly allies. The information was also to aid the Foreign Office in producing propaganda pamphlets for dissemination to the enemy's citizens.

From 4 September 1939, the day after war was declared, until its dissolution in March 1946, the ministry was there to ensure the people read and heard the right sort of stuff. The focus of this chapter is on how the ministry controlled what the people of Britain read, watched and heard.

In June 1940, an emergency regulation was introduced that made it an offence to publish any war-related 'report or statement which was likely to cause alarm or despondency'. Breaching the regulations was punishable by fines of up to £50. Initially, the press were, understandably, far from enamored with the idea of censorship. Ultimately, however, it was deemed necessary to protect the morale of the Home Front and security of the country as a whole.

Like citizens, news editors were subject to regulations under the Emergency Powers Act, which made it an offence to communicate or publish any information that might be useful to the enemy. The problem was that, unlike their readers, editors also had a responsibility to keep people informed. The principle was that only information regarding military matters, or that which might be of use to the enemy, could not be reported. But newspapers were still able to report facts, comments and opinions. This, of course, yielded a large grey area. For example, where does opinion become defeatism that could possibly damage morale and thereby aid the enemy?

In practice, censorship took several forms. For example, articles on air raids would focus on rescue efforts and stories of bravery and courage, and were devoid of such details as death tolls and destruction. In fact, it was not allowed to report the actual number of fatalities when more than twelve people were killed in an incident. It is also worth noting that reports of raids rarely include much detail of where the bombs had actually fallen. The most specific a story might get is to say 'a London borough', rather than naming the particular district.

This was to keep the enemy, who would invariably have been getting copies of British newspapers, from knowing exactly where they had hit. Such details could aid them in planning future raids. Papers were also told which pictures they could use. The ministry preferred shots of authorities clearing wreckage and helping people, to ones showing desolation and despair. The ministry's message to the people was fairly simple to ascertain: 'We know there is a war on but chin up.'

One example of a story censored by the government was that of the arrival on British soil of Rudolf Hess on 10 May 1941, coincidentally the last night of the Blitz. As London was suffering one of its worst attacks, Hess, who was Hitler's deputy, parachuted out of his Messerschmitt fighter aircraft over Scotland, in the hope of securing peace talks with the British government. He was taken to London, but the press was banned from reporting his presence until two days later when his flight to Britain was reported by German Radio.

Even then, the papers were still barred from saying Hess was in Britain to talk peace, amid fears that many beleaguered Brits, worn down by months of attacks, would clamour to make a deal. The press could report that Hess was 'talking freely', but not what he was talking freely about, Angus Calder noted.

Public weather forecasts were also banned, as they could in theory be of help to the enemy. Even weather from the previous ten days was not to be reported, lest it give the invaders valuable information about the state of Britain. In 1940, with the Germans having reached the French coast and able to see the cliffs at Dover and therefore what the weather was doing, weather reports for the Straits of Dover could be reported. People across the country, therefore, could learn if it was raining in the English Channel, but not what the weather had in store for wherever they were, or even what the weather had been doing in the days before.

Another example of censorship was the news coverage later in the war of the V-1 and V-2 flying bombs. Initially, there was a total ban on reporting the V-1s hitting London, an arrangement that at first had the support of the Newspaper and Periodical Emergency Council, a body made up of newspaper editors. It was felt that reporting on the V-1s and the damage they caused would only provide valuable information to the Germans, thereby aiding them with improving their targeting. As more rockets arrived, however, resentment grew.

'The ban became intolerable', wrote former BBC war correspondent John Simpson in his 2010-work, *Unreliable Sources: How the 20th Century was Reported*. Eventually, Winston Churchill negated the restriction by giving a full account of V-1 activity in the House of Commons in July.

The ban was back in place again, however, for the V-2. The first impact of one was explained away as a gas explosion. This time the newspapers made representations to have the ban on reporting lifted. John Simpson continues on the subject:

> The worst thing about censorship is that if newspapers and radio cease to tell them what they know is true, people lose their belief in anything they are told officially and rumours, no matter how wild, take over. This happened now.

Realising that the censorship of V-2 reports was damaging morale, the government acquiesced a little. Reports could be published as long as they were kept vague and were only released several days after the event. Simpson writes:

> The Ministry of War was convinced that this fooled the Germans and prevented them from improving the effectiveness of the V-2. But the credibility of the newspapers and BBC suffered as hugely destructive explosions, which people saw with their own eyes, went unreported. Such feelings fostered a suspicion of officialdom and the press, which the British government had tried to avoid.

'Censorship was touted as a way to prevent the leakage of military information to the enemy', wrote Amy Helen Bell in *London Was Ours*, 'though government agencies extended censorship beyond military matters in an attempt to assess and direct public opinion.'

She cites an editor working for the Ministry of Information, whose job it was to edit copy for the press. Each day a set of rules called 'Stops and Releases' would be read aloud in the office. This included not referencing certain types of bomb, being vague about the number of casualties, for example thirty-five would be replaced by the word 'some', while 'considerable' became a euphemism for a major incident.

Bell also describes the situation for photographers wanting to capture London on film during and after raids: 'Photographs of London during the Blitz were heavily censored to protect civilian morale and to conceal from the Germans information about the success of their raids.'

Only those with permits from the Ministry of Information were allowed to take photographs. To acquire a permit, photographers had to be accredited to a bona fide body, such as a newspaper company or official agency.

Before pictures could be published, they had to be seen by the ministry's censors. To speed up the process, many photographers would actually self-censor their own work, although there were also cases where people at the scene of an incident would censor the picture there. For example, they might remonstrate with a photographer they deemed to be taking an inappropriate picture. Bell describes one photographer who was challenged by one 'officious passer-by' as he attempted to take pictures of a wax head among the ruins of a hairdresser's shop. The passer-by said the photographing of heads, wax or otherwise, 'wasn't right'. The incident ended with a police constable being called and the photographer being escorted away from the scene.

The BBC too, was censored, although the organisation put up strong resistance to any kind of government interference in Auntie's independence.

'It seems to me that the only way to strengthen the morale of the people whose morale is worth strengthening, is to tell them the truth, and nothing but the truth, even if the truth is horrible', wrote R.T. Clark, the news editor of the Home Service in an internal memo.

The organisation was in a difficult position. It saw its independence threatened, particularly at the start of the war, by the government's wishes to use the national broadcaster to promote propaganda and to counter that being issued by the enemy.

The BBC, however, argued that its audience should be told the truth about what was going on, rather than getting filtered and skewed information.

'In the long run, a trusted news source for audiences at home and abroad would be a more potent weapon,' said a BBC historian on the organisation's website.

Desmond Hawkins, a wartime broadcaster for the BBC, said:

> The BBC couldn't, in wartime, be independent; it would be childish
> to think that there were not ultimate sanctions that the nation had

to reserve to itself. But nor was the BBC dependent, it stood on a declared and understood position, it was its own man on the terms that were possible.

It was agreed that the BBC should seek to report events truthfully and accurately, but not in such detail as to endanger the civilian population or jeopardise operations. The result was that the BBC did report setbacks as well as successes. Hawkins continues:

> It would say, for instance, that bombs had fallen and that there were casualties. But precise number of casualties and the location and time of a bombing would often be withheld, so that the enemy would not know which of its missions had found the target.

Even then, the BBC was still open to criticism from those who wanted to use it as the government's propaganda machine. Winston Churchill had fallen out with the organisation while he was chancellor during the 1926 General Strike. Against his wishes, the broadcaster had aired the statements of the strikers. Recalling that incident during the Second World War, Churchill referred to the BBC as 'the enemy within the gates, doing more harm than good.'

But the BBC was vitally important to the public. Its news sections, six scheduled per day between seven in the morning and midnight, were listened to by millions.

'It is impossible to exaggerate the impact of the BBC's wartime news,' said Tom Hickman in *What Did You Do in the War, Auntie*. 'Newspapers were thin because, like everything, paper was rationed, and they could not match radio's fast reflexes.'

On the point of paper rationing, in his memoirs John Sweetland, who was 12 at the start of the war, recalled going on paper collection rounds:

> This involved making a nuisance of myself knocking on front doors and asking for newspapers and magazines, which were carted away to a spare room on the estate to join an ever-growing mountain; a rich source of comics and other publications of interest.

On Friday, 1 September 1939, two days before war was declared, the BBC merged all of its regional radio output into one channel, the Home Service. The organisation also kept its World Service running throughout the war.

The reasoning for creating a Home Service was twofold. Firstly, it would stop the aerial German raiders being able to work out where they were and therefore able to target certain towns or cities. Secondly, it meant the public, in theory at least, were all listening to the same broadcasts, which made for much quicker and simpler dissemination of important information. And the BBC was very important.

'Out of a total population of 48 million, probably as many as 40 million were listening to the BBC', wrote historian Juliet Gardiner in her 2004-work *Wartime Britain 1939–1945*.

At first, the Home Service was not a great success. It was overloaded with dull messages from the Ministry of Information about rationing, national savings and economising on fuel. There were dull news bulletins and serious music to reflect the nation being at war. Realising, however, that many were instead choosing to tune into foreign broadcasts, such as that of Lord Haw-Haw on Radio Hamburg, new programmes were introduced that attracted listeners back. *It's That Man Again*, a comedy, was one such show, which proved highly popular with the listening public. Some 14 million people tuned into *ITMA*, while 17 million regularly listened to the nine o'clock news every night.

Eventually, even *Saturday Night Theatre*, a weekly drama show that started in 1943, pulled in 10 million or so listeners. Another popular programme was *The Kitchen Front*, a five-minute long broadcast on every day at 8.15 am. This was timed so that housewives could listen to it, and get tips and advice on what they should be cooking before they headed out to the shops. There was a news bulletin on the hour every hour, the most popular of which being the nine o'clock news in the evening.

There were a few interesting changes to the way the BBC broadcast during the Second World War. One was the way newsreaders presented themselves. Previously, they would have used a nickname, but now they started using their own names. This was part of the plan to guard against Hitler seizing the BBC and using it to broadcast false information. Also, at the beginning of the war the BBC relied on reports from agencies. By the end of the conflict, the BBC had several of its own correspondents covering the war, most famously perhaps Richard Dimbleby. The organisation had forty-eight correspondents covering D-Day in June 1944. Simpson writes:

> The war really made the BBC. It had become the country's, and often the outside world's, most trusted source of news. The old rules about relying solely on news agencies for its reporting were set aside. Increasingly it had sent two- or three-man recording teams into the front line.

At the start of the war, the organisation employed 5,100 people. By the end of March 1942, Auntie's staff numbered almost 12,000.

The BBC compiled its own reports for broadcast, but, according to Tom Hickman, it was 'officially guided' by the Ministry of Information. BBC staff were seconded to the ministry and ministry men were always present in the BBC newsroom. Before a script could be broadcast it needed to pass two censors. The first focused on the security of the armed services, the other, on the morale of the nation. Hickman wrote:

> No script could be broadcast unless it bore both stamps. Among the ground rules of censorship were that the names of regiments, the numbers of troops or planes and precise geographic locations were never given, nor were the whereabouts of members of the Cabinet and the Royal family. The weather was never mentioned either, in case it revealed the conditions for bombing.

This did verge on the ridiculous, particularly during one Oxford and Cambridge boat race. The commentator was not allowed to say that he could not see how far ahead Cambridge were because the sun was in his eyes.

The BBC, however, was not the only broadcaster. Wireless listeners were also able to pick up channels from abroad. One of the most infamous radio voices was that of William Joyce, nicknamed Lord Haw-Haw, an American-Irish Briton who, in his well-spoken English accent, would expound the virtues of the Nazi regime and attempt to undermine the morale of the British people. His programmes would start with the cry 'Germany calling, Germany calling'. He would then set out to contradict what was being reported by the British press, replacing it with Nazi propaganda.

His broadcasts, which carried on throughout the war, came first from Berlin in September 1939, then Luxembourg, and finally Hamburg. He was arrested near the Danish border a short time after the end of the war. He was subsequently found guilty of three counts of treason and hanged on 3 January 1946 at Wandsworth Prison. He was 39 years old.

Though people were discouraged from listening to his broadcasts, they did prove very popular with an estimated six-million regular listeners – a sixth of the listening public – and a further eighteen-million occasional ones. Joyce was not the only Nazi propagandist to be heard on England's wireless sets, but he is arguably the most famous.

As well as the Home Service, from 1940 to 1944 the BBC also broadcast the *Forces Programme* – later the *General Forces Programme* – to entertain the troops. This consisted of morale-boosting music and shows aimed at keeping the boys entertained in between their engagements with the enemy. The Home Service actually stayed on the air until 1967, when it became Radio Four. Even now, Radio Four has not forgotten its roots in keeping the public informed of military matters.

According to David Hendy in *Life On The Air: A History Of Radio Four*, in the event of a nuclear attack the station will be the 'last voice of authority we hear before Armageddon arrives'.

'It's continuity announcer', Hendy wrote, 'ensconced in a bunker offering crumbs of comfort in hushed but elegant tones when all other broadcasters have been atomized into silence.'

The BBC was criticised for the way it presented the news, and in particular for the way reports would optimistically focus on the positives of an event, and somewhat gloss over any unpleasantness or negativity.

In a letter to *The Times* in February 1942, Winchester MP Gerald Palmer expressed his dissatisfaction with the way war news was being reported, especially with the downplaying of German successes. He wrote:

> Before the war the British public may have had an unfortunate taste for pleasant soporifics but the authorities responsible for official and semi-official news today seem to be ignorant of the fact that that taste has long been outgrown. An appeal to the fighting spirit of this country will never fail as long as there is confidence that it is based on facts; but half-truths, which seek to minimise the facts or gloss over defeat, can result only in confusion, lack of effort and even exasperation.

Another letter writer to *The Times*, H.B. Turle, said the presentation of the news would only engender complacency among the people. He was also referring to speeches made by MPs, which were prefaced by such statements as 'while ultimate victory is certain', when he wrote:

> It is as though we were living through the pages of a book in which Britain is the hero who will infallibly triumph in the last chapter. But alas! The present times are not fiction, they are grim reality and victory is not certain – it must be won.

One heavily censored report of the Allies' failed assault on Dieppe in 1942 caused much ire – although to be fair, it was not just the BBC who published deceptive stories on the affair. Even the reporter behind the story, Frank Gillard, was said to be disgusted with it. More than 3,000 Canadians had been killed, but you would not have known that from the heavily censored reports, which painted the raid as a valuable and successful learning experience.

In his diaries, on 22 August 1942, George Orwell noted how the story of the raid had been spun:

> David Astor (a journalist who had witnessed the raid) was very damning about the Dieppe raid, which he saw at more or less close quarters and which he says was an almost complete failure, except for the heavy destruction of German fighter planes, which was not part of the plan. He says that the affair was definitely misrepresented in the press and is now being misrepresented in the reports to the PM. About twenty to thirty tanks were landed but none were got off again. The newspaper photos which showed tanks apparently being brought back to England were intentionally misleading.

Some, however, realised the tricky position the BBC was in, recognising that it verged on them being damned if they did and damned if they did not. In a letter to *The Times*, Eden Phillpotts wrote:

> Their exceedingly difficult task demands obvious need to hold the scales evenly between successes and setbacks. For baldly to announce items of utmost gravity and disappointment, and make no effort to gild the pill when it is reasonable to do so, would instantly arouse adverse criticism. Then your correspondents must complain that the silver lining of every cloud was consistently ignored by the BBC and the worst possible interpretation set upon events.

Another reader, EW Adams, wrote: 'There is a very nice and very difficult balance to be kept by so presenting news that on the one hand complacency is not fostered and on the other hand doubt and despondency are not engendered.'

Others were simply unhappy with the use of reports from correspondents recorded out in the field, saying background battlefield noise rendered some parts inaudible.

'It was like having to read an important letter so badly written that in trying to decipher the script one missed the meaning', wrote EJ Phillips to

The Times. 'What possible advantage is there in this method of broadcasting? It is the report we want to hear, not the distorted voice of the reporter.'

That their reports focused mainly on positives was not the fault of the journalists. With the government censors reading, editing and approving the copy of the correspondents before it was published, the news that the public read was bound to be skewed.

'Journalists' stories usually combine elements that are broadly positive with others that are negative', wrote John Simpson. 'In wartime the censors usually cut out the negative things with the result that the reporting tends to glow with unalloyed optimism.'

Although spirits were rising with the end of the war seemingly approaching, the news still had the capability of alarming the citizens. One of the most shocking revelations was the discovery of the concentration camps on the continent, images of which were seen by millions of Britons at the cinemas.

John Sweetland, by this point a 17-year-old civil servant, was clearly shaken by the 'astounding revelations of the vile acts perpetrated at Belsen', a camp in southern Germany where some 70,000 people died. British troops liberated the camp on 15 April 1945. They found 60,000 prisoners inside, many starved and on the brink of death. They also found 13,000 bodies strewn around the camp, left where they had died.

Sweetland wrote of the moment news of the liberation was screened:

The full cinema went completely quiet as the newsreel progressed save for the gasps and moans of horror from the audience. Mother turned to me with tears streaming down her face and, with choking voice, she just said to me, 'You shouldn't have to see such things.'

Bunty recalls:

At that point we did not know what the Germans had really been doing. I remember though that when people started to realise the real horror of what had been happening, we all knew that the suffering we had been through was for a very just cause, it was impossible to comprehend the enormity of the Nazi's actions, it was just horrible.

Chapter Eleven

Troubles of a Wartime Teenager

Being a teenager is tough. Just because there is a war on it does not mean all the other dramas and dilemmas of adolescence disappear.

In her diaries from 1943, Bunty complains of her weight, the stress of exams, the frustration of friends and the attraction of the opposite sex, as much as she discusses the actual war. She wrote on Wednesday, 13 January:

> In afternoon kept appointment at Dr Browns. Have lost no weight. Am not surprised after Christmas. He says fatness definitely due to diet, not glands. Am rather relieved about this and have seriously told myself for millionth time to eat less! Had a long walk with Midge in afternoon and ate light dinner. Wonder how long this will last!

The following day she wrote: 'I managed to carry out my non-fat-eating campaign today quite successfully. Oh please let me have enough will to really get results this time!'

By the Friday, she was struggling: 'Kept to diet quite well again today, but had one or two bad moments; one Cornish pasty at lunchtime and ginger cake in the evening. Oh! to be the streamline type!!'

Another entry, this time from Monday, 8 March, shows another valiant attempt was being made to slim down:

> Felt pretty rotten today but think it's because I tried to exist on Vitawheat for breakfast and lunch. I just can't diet but guess I shall never give up trying 'til I lose several stone! Which in itself would be a miracle.

Exams and revision for them were also a perennial problem for Bunty. On Monday, 18 January, after writing about air raids, she noted: 'This afternoon we had Pathology and theory three-monthly test. Papers were really very easy but I'm afraid I muffed them.'

And again the following day she had more exam-related woe:

> Anatomy and physiology paper this afternoon which, like yesterday's, was not really difficult but fear I haven't answered very well. I'd finished about half an hour too soon which looks rather as if my answers were too brief.

As it turned out, she did quite well, scoring the second-highest mark in the class for her anatomy and physiology papers, and finishing fourth in the pathology and theory exam. This was not a reason to celebrate though.

'In spite of these high placings my marks were nothing to be proud of', she wrote. 'Forty-nine/eighty for first paper and fifty/eighty for second, which just shows how low the standard of our set is at present! However, it's a great relief to know I'm not the worst.'

And even in her last entry on Thursday, 10 June, exams are still causing a nuisance:

> Had a theory test in the afternoon for which I did very little work – none in fact. I was resigned to a boring time being able to write nothing. However it wasn't quite so bad as I expected, that is I wrote a good deal, but probably all wrong.

Bunty also complained of being tired. Of course, teenagers are a notoriously tired group – it seems to be an established fact that they need plenty of sleep. In fact, the National Sleep Foundation claims teens need between eight and ten hours of sleep of a night in order to fully function when awake. According to Nationwide Children, the magic number is nine-and-a-quarter hours exactly. Living in London during the Blitz, however, was far from conducive for a good night's sleep. Even if there were no German raiders, there were still plenty of false alarms to keep Londoners from their slumber.

Naturally, the war was also in the thoughts of many young people. Teenagers in the run up to the war had to contend with disputes over the rights and wrongs of conflict with their parents and relations who had some twenty years previously lived through the world's worst war.

One *Mass Observer* noted several heated debates with his older acquaintances as war loomed and then commenced in 1939. He noted disagreements over the amount of blame that should be levelled at the Germans, his aunt arguing that they had betrayed the post-First World War peace agreements by rearming. He argued that Hitler's rise to power was thanks to the ill treatment Germany suffered at the hands of the Allies in the post-war years. If his views are anything to go by, many young people saw war as both unwanted and unavoidable. The threat Hitler posed was just too great to ignore. *The Mass Observer*'s hatred was not of the Germans, but rather of the rise and ambitions of Adolf Hitler. No reasonable person would be unafraid of war, but it was an inevitability that it needed to be fought.

The war also contributed to age-old problems faced by teenagers, such as a lack of purpose and direction. Some young people, for example, found themselves in limbo, waiting to be called up. The 19-year-old *Mass Observer* had his application to become an air-raid warden rejected because of his age. It was unfair, he said, because no employers would take on men of that age as they were so close to military age and liable to be called up – being a warden was something with which they could fill their time.

Perhaps one of the biggest grievances for young men in particular was the arrival of thousands of love rivals from the United States. By the end of spring 1944, 1,421,000 troops from elsewhere were in Britain on their way to the various fronts. The vast majority of these were the American GIs, nicknamed after the words 'Government Issue' stamped or emblazoned onto their equipment.

'As young men, our noses were put out of joint by American servicemen crowding out the West End and attracting the girls with their money and nylon stockings, with which we couldn't compete', wrote John Sweetland, who was 17 in 1945.

The problem for the young Englishmen was their American counterparts were paid more, had access to luxuries such as sweets, cosmetics and clothes, and were an attractive option for young women. 'Overpaid, oversexed and over here', was the saying used by many and popularised by comedian Tommy Trinder.

'It is difficult to go anywhere in London without having the feeling that Britain is now occupied territory', is how George Orwell felt in 1943.

'To British women, the arrival of the Americans was a bright flash of excitement after nearly three years of blackout and Blitz', wrote John Costello in *Virtue Under Fire*, a study of how the war affected social and sexual attitudes. 'It seemed to many that these strapping, well-fed and confident young men had stepped straight out of a Hollywood movie.'

Doris Scott, in her memoirs in *Forgotten Voices of the Second World War*, said:

> The Americans were a jolly and friendly crowd. It was like
> Hollywood come to life. Many girls were bowled over by them and

I think the British soldiers didn't like it very much. The reserve of the English was in sharp contrast to their friendly 'got any gum, chum?' way of talking. They certainly made an impact.

The American servicemen were issued with instruction booklets offering advice on how best to ingratiate themselves with the natives:

The British dislike bragging and showing off. American soldiers' pay is the highest in the world, when pay day comes it would be sound practice to learn to spend your money according to British standards. They won't think any better of you for throwing money around. You are higher paid than the British Tommy, don't rub it in. Play fair with him, he can be a pal in need. Two actions on your part will slow up the friendship – swiping his girl and not appreciating that his army has been up against it.

The guide, which has been reproduced by the Bodleian Library, also urges the GIs to be sensible and sensitive to the fact that Britain has been wrapped up in a war since 1939:

Britain may look a little shop-worn and grimy, the British people are anxious to have you know that you are not seeing their country at its best. The houses have not been painted because factories are not making paint – they're making planes. The famous English gardens and parks are either unkempt because there are no men to take care of them, or they are being used to grow needed vegetables. It is always impolite to criticise your hosts, it is militarily stupid to insult your allies. So stop and think before you sound off about lukewarm beer, cold boiled potatoes or the way English cigarettes taste.

Bunty had plenty of opportunities to meet young men from around the world as, during the war, the Leatherdale family house on Croxted Road became a port of call for many passing servicemen. She recalls:

We had relatives in New Zealand who would recommend us as a place to visit to their friends. I think it was nice for these young men who had left behind their homes and family to go and fight a war to have somewhere friendly they could visit. They would come round for dinner and were always very pleasant and good fun.

For a teenage girl, meeting young men from across the other side of the world would have been an exciting time, even if it was because they were coming to fight. London was swelling with foreigners passing through on their way to the European front, as well as refugees fleeing the war.

Two such characters in Bunty's world were Texas Dan, an American serviceman acquaintance of her best friend Nancy, and Gordon Russell, a member of the Royal New Zealand Navy, who had stayed with the Leatherdales, and with whom Bunty maintained a correspondence. On one occasion, Texas Dan agreed to take Bunty, Nancy and their friend Margery out to a show.

'I thought it very gallant of Texas to take three girls out but he seemed to quite enjoy the situation!' she later wrote.

Opportunities to meet new and interesting folk abounded. Take her Sunday cycling trip to Surrey in February 1943 for example. She had caught the train to Dorking together with Nancy and Peggy, from where the trio cycled to Guildford. Bunty writes:

> Two Canadian soldiers also spending their afternoon cycling aimlessly around the countryside joined us and guided us to a pleasant guest-house where we enjoyed a delicious tea and much joking and laughing. Learnt that soldiers were called Bill Ryan and Archie, the former being my favourite.

Two days later she wrote a letter to Bill Ryan, although with typical teenage misgivings she said: 'Bet I live to regret it!'

A week or two later she received a reply, and although she expresses no feelings about it, the fact is that it was the first thing she wrote down in her diary entry that day, perhaps giving some indication of the importance it had for her.

Dances provided opportunities to meet young gentlemen, and though they were rarer than in pre-war years, Bunty still attended several during her diary days. On Tuesday, 30 March 1943, she was invited to one such gathering at Ivyholme, a boarding house at Dulwich College.

Although reluctant to go as it was a week of yet more exams, go she did and, as she notes in the following day's diary, it was well worth the effort:

> Well the dance has been fun - great fun! Why does it always happen that when an arrangement is 'last moment' and not much looked forward to its invariably a success. Met two pleasant boys – Monty

somebody and Gordon Carry. What's more, they seemed to like me! I danced quite a lot, and talked a good deal, and was in a much more confident mood when I left than when I arrived! Gordon C. walked home with me. He lives in Edinburgh and is one of the Ivyholme students that is studying Chinese or Japanese – I can't remember which. He is going home in a few days' time for a month's holiday.

The next day she was invited out again by the same group and this time got to know Monty a bit better:

When I arrived I renewed my acquaintance with Monty, we got on very well together and the result was another highly successful evening! Sardines and murder were the main games – so like those old parties we gave when at school. The proportions were rather in our favour that is about five girls and twenty-five boys! Monty took me home and my opinion of him went up the longer I was with him. It's a pity he has finished his course at Dulwich.

Sadly, as his course was finishing, Monty was due to leave London soon.

'I am feeling increasingly sorry that I didn't meet Monty earlier on during his period in Dulwich', Bunty wrote in her diary. 'Just my luck that it should be the last two days of his course! Wrote to him re my cigarette lighter!' This last part, she later admitted to me, was something of a ruse to make contact with him:

'I probably told a little white lie, something like "did I leave my cigarette lighter with you?" I think I was probably being a bit devious, making up an excuse to see him again.'

A few days later she received a reply: 'Started the day well by receiving an answer from Monty', she wrote, adding, 'It was a very satisfactory letter. Wrote to Monty in the evening telling him that I had found my lighter!'

In April, Bunty was contacted by another male friend and, as her diary recounts, it ended in a pleasant evening out at the Ritz:

Had a marvellous 'surprise' evening – Vernon Small old school pal of Dudley Bird's I met about a year ago, phoned and arranged to meet me. I remembered so little about him that I was rather dubious about the outcome of the arrangement, but my doubts were all ill-founded. With two friends of his – an American pilot and his girlfriend Phyllis – the four of us dined at Shephards Tavern off

Piccadilly then went on a refined 'pub crawl'. I had my first view of inside The Ritz, and various other establishments couldn't believe it was me out with two such good looking officers!

The following day her happiness at the previous evening's frivolity remained, and she ended her diary entry: 'The likelihood of seeing Vernon was very remote but I must confess I had hoped.'

While she was meeting new people, however, she also had to contend with the loss of old friends – some just absent, others never to return. On Saturday, 20 March, she attended a dance with some friends, which, though enjoyable, was also notable for the lack of pre-war dancing partners:

'It was all very reminiscent of the marvellous pre-war dances we had, but Donald's present absence was very prominent.'

Donald had been part of her circle of friends before the war, another member of whom was Gordon, whose letters to Bunty usually met with an excited entry in her diary.

On 8 May 1945, the war in Europe was over as Victory in Europe (VE) Day was celebrated. Though joyous the war was over, many teenagers felt conflicting emotions. John Sweetland and his friend Gus attended the VE Day parties in the West End, but neither felt like celebrating. Sweetland wrote:

The war had begun when I was eleven and now, being seventeen, the whole of those six years, despite every hardship, had been the only real and normal life that I could recognise. Peacetime presented a prospect of the great unknown in which the unity of wartime would vanish. So it was that I felt a complete outsider, observing only the dancing, singing and general merrymaking taking place in the West End. Servicemen would now rightly look forward to a return to civilian life, with the promise of a better life than the one they had left. But with the war in the Far East not yet over, Gus and I had to await our call-up to the services and I, as a temporary civil servant, would be without a job to return to, if and when I did.

For many young people then, peacetime offered just as many fraught decisions as the war did, although arguably much less fatal ones.

Chapter Twelve

Who was Bunty?

For the first six months of 1943, Glennis Amy Leatherdale kept a diary. Over the following pages, you will get to read it.

First though, it is best if we learn who she was. To this end, I spent a rather rainy afternoon in the summer of 2016 in my grandmother's living room, gleaning her potted history. At various points during our interview, she would pause mid-sentence, pull herself up out of her chair and totter over to the window. She would bash on the window with a wooden spoon at the unwanted pigeons and crows availing themselves of her bird-feeder tables. The spoon, it's worth noting, is permanently left there for exactly that purpose. Alternatively, she might scurry off into the neighbouring room to delve into various plastic bags or drawers to find bits of paper or old photographs that she thought might be of use to me.

Born above her family's bakery in south London on 2 February 1924, she was officially named Glennis, but came to be known to all her friends and family as Bunty, a popular nickname at the time, derived from the 1921 film *Bunty Pulls the Strings*. Perhaps Glennis's family felt she was acting like the eponymous character.

The Leatherdales were well-off, not rich exactly, but certainly comfortable thanks to the bakery run by her father Alfred. His father had started the company in 1870 by selling his homemade bread from a barrow. At its peak, the Leatherdale Bakery had twelve shops around London, and also sold bread in Harrods.

'It started off in such a very humble way but finished up with a chain of shops and a very strong reputation,' Bunty recalled.

The main bakery was at 32 Kennington Lane, and it was here that Bunty was born. She was the second child of Alfred and Gertrude Leatherdale, her brother Peter having arrived four years earlier.

Soon after her birth, her parents decided to buy a proper family home rather than raise them in the flat above the Kennington Lane bakery where they had been living.

'Kennington was a bit low key,' recalls Bunty some ninety years on, 'that's why we moved to Dulwich.'

Their Dulwich home was on Croxted Road. It was a large Edwardian house with a long back garden big enough for a tennis court and vegetable patch. The garden was also home for Alfred's collection of chickens, known as his Little Ladies. They were a vital source of eggs for the family during the years of rationing.

They could afford to send their two children to private school. Peter was educated at Dulwich College, and Bunty first at Dulwich High School and then Streatham Hill High School.

'Neither of my parents had had much education and they wanted to do the best for their children,' Bunty said. 'My father left school at fifteen because his mother died, she had wanted him to stay at school but his father wanted him to get into the business.'

Though her father's firm was a success, the young Bunty was hesitant to tell her school friends his profession:

> In those days, being in a trade like my father was very looked down upon and I was very hesitant to tell any of my friends at school that I was a baker's daughter. All the other students were the daughters of doctors and lawyers. I did not want them to know I was only a baker's daughter. It seems absurd now. He was a successful businessman. There was certainly nothing to be ashamed of, but back then these things seemed important.

She was 15 when war broke out, bringing her education to an abrupt end. Fortunately, Bunty was attending classes a year above her age group, so, in the summer before, she was able to take and gain her National Certificate. Had she been with her own age group, war would have intervened and she would never have passed it. To this day, she is very grateful she did get the qualification as it ultimately allowed her to train for and get her dream career – physiotherapy.

'I do consider myself very lucky,' she said. 'Of course at the time I did not realise it, I had no idea that I was not going to go back to school.'

After war was declared in September 1939, her school closed and its inhabitants – both students and staff – evacuated. Bunty did not go with them, saying:

> I did not want to go. I didn't want to leave London. There was a suggestion I should go and spend the war with family in New Zealand but there was no way I was going to let that happen as I

didn't want to leave my home and parents. I was not concerned about being hurt or anything. I just did not want to go. It would have been awful to be so far away from them and not knowing what was happening to them. No, I wanted to stay in London, and I'm very glad I did.

She did get out of London occasionally. The mother of a friend, Shirley Massey, had taken a home in the Welsh town of Balla in which to live for the duration of the war. Bunty visited. She also went on holidays – as her diary attests – but fundamentally, London was home for the entirety of the war.

London in wartime was an experience she said she would have been devastated to miss:

> It was a tremendous experience for me being in London during those years of the war. I suppose I was young enough not to really be affected by it, but looking back now I think it must have been horrific for my parents. They had already lived through one war, now they were having to do it again, but this time with two children who were at the age where they could be called up. It must have been really awful for them. It did not mean the same to me as it did to them. My father had been in the trenches, and my poor mother had had to live with the knowledge that her fiancée was away at war and could be seriously injured or killed at any moment. Then there was peace and he came home, but now, just twenty years later, we were at war again and she could have faced losing her children.

For Bunty, wartime London proved surprisingly exhilarating, saying:

> It wasn't all doom and gloom. We still managed to go to the theatre and the cinema. There was an exciting atmosphere in the city. Due to the age I was at then I didn't really worry. It was a lot to do with the age group you were in really. As I say, it was a lot more worrying for my parents having children old enough to be in it; Peter in the RAF and me in the hospital in central London. To me it was a very stimulating time, which I'm very glad I went through. It gave me a rather unpleasant attitude towards whingers today. You just think, 'for goodness sake stop moaning'. It would have been a very different country that people grew up in if the Germans had won the war.

We felt safe down in our cellar at night. There were times when it was almost every night. When we had New Zealand cousin friends staying, they would come down. It would be quite a jolly party there. On one night, there was a stick of bombs fell one each side of the house and the whole house shook, a load of plaster fell on us. But it didn't wake our New Zealand navy friends – they must have been used to it. I remember sometimes having a skeleton down there to help me with my anatomy studies while I was training to be a physiotherapist. This was a real human skeleton, you understand, not made of plastic. My father was not too happy. 'It's bad enough we are being bombed let alone having you fiddle with a corpse during it all,' he said. I only recently found out that, after we had finished with them, those bones were given back to the family of the person that died to be given a full funeral. I had never thought about what happened to them.

With her school closed, Bunty needed to find something to do. She wanted to be a physiotherapist but needed to wait until she was 18 before she could commence with her training. So, in the meantime, she enrolled at a Pitman's College to learn shorthand and typing. She subsequently found herself doing secretarial work in a bank.

'I think it was a bit of nepotism that got me the job there,' she said. 'My father had an account with them and I'm fairly sure they took me on as a favour to him.'

She enjoyed her time at the bank, although she had to contend with the fact that she was probably one of the first women employed there: 'I was only a very lowly position, but all the men that worked there treated me with great respect and reverence. I don't think they were used to working with a woman.'

Air raids would be spent down in the bank's safe room.

Finally, at the age of 18, Bunty signed up for a physiotherapy training course at Guy's Hospital. She said:

I had read an article on healing hands and I liked the sound of it, so I knew exactly what I wanted to do. As I said, it was providential I had the National Certificate – you had to have it to do the course. I don't know what I would have done if I hadn't had it. You didn't go to university or anything. You were in at the deep end right from the beginning. You treated patients right from the beginning under supervision.

Bunty mostly treated injured servicemen at Guy's and Orpington, but she also had to look after impoverished children from London's bomb-battered slums.

'A lot of the little children in London suffered from rickets because they didn't get enough sunshine,' she said. 'We used to treat them with a long strip of ultra-violet light.'

Of course, the war intruded massively on her life, as it did for all Londoners. She recalled several incidents and their aftermaths:

> On one occasion a V-1 rocket had hit the Smarts' (family friends) house. The mother had been killed so the father and young people came to live with us. That was what one did – you just helped out your neighbours, and they came and used your home. I don't remember ever being out in air raids. There were more at night than during the day so I was at home. I didn't really do anything special to be prepared. I just went to bed as normal and then, if the siren sounded, I would put on a dressing gown and go down to the cellar. You usually had plenty of warning; it was only with the V-2 rockets where there was never any warning. I remember a rocket came once while I was still upstairs. That landed just behind us on a church. The first I knew of it was the sound of impact. All the other times you got the warning siren. You didn't panic. It was all just a part of life.

Although her home emerged unscathed, Bunty did see the effects of the raids:

> When I was working at the bank in City Road I used to get the bus to the Oval and then the tube. One night after a fire raid, there were no buses, so I had to walk to the Oval through Brixton. I was stepping over hoses and rubble. You could still smell all the smoke and stuff in the air. Then, when I was at Guy's, I would go on the train from West Dulwich station up to London Bridge. There was one occasion when bombs fell right beside the line. The train had to stop and we were told none of us were allowed to get out. We had little choice but to sit there and wait. We were left there watching the aftermath of bombs falling on houses and people being brought out. That was a pretty awful experience. Eventually they said we could get out and walk along the railway line to the next station.

Bunty also came face to face with those seeking shelter on the London underground:

> Once you were down in the tube, you felt safe. There were all these people who had slept the night down there. They were just lying on sorts of blankets and things. A lot of them would do that every night as it was where they felt safest.

Being a trainee physiotherapist meant Bunty was in a 'reserved occupation', so she was not available to be called up. Her brother Peter was an engineer and he did join the war effort, plying his trade for the RAF. He too would have been exempt from conscription, as working in a bakery, which he was also doing, was classed as reserved. He followed the example his father set more than twenty years before, however, and signed up anyway.

In the First World War, Alfred's bakery business meant he did not have to go the front, but go he did, leaving the bakery to be run by his older brother Chris. He saw a great deal of action in the trenches, including at the Battle of the Somme, before a shrapnel wound to his hand put paid to his war service. Medics had wanted to amputate, but he was insistent on keeping his wounded hand so he could resume his work as a baker. He never really regained full mobility of his left hand, but he was still able to bake and run the business his father had started.

Having seen the horrors of the trenches, Alfred now had to live through the wanton destruction of his home city, and the loss of many friends and strangers. These, however were all concerns far from the consciousness of his young daughter. Bunty just kept on living during the war, her memories positive as well as negative:

> I experienced the Blitz spirit first hand. It was the fact that we had lived through and experienced the Blitz, but it hadn't got us down – it made us all tougher. The Germans hoped bombing us would want us to end the war, but it didn't. In fact, it had the opposite effect. It galvanised us and made us want to fight even more.
>
> Of course, at that time we did not really know the full horrors of the Nazi regime, and of the awful concentration camps. Everybody was shocked and horrified when that truth emerged. We realised more than ever that it was an essential war and a war that had to be won. Otherwise we would have been a Nazi-dominated country,

and all the Jews here would have been killed and goodness knows what else. We were always pretty positive we would win the war. Obviously, certain battles that were won, like El Alamein, made us think we would win it. Perhaps my parents thought differently, but certainly people my age never thought we would lose it.

Chapter Thirteen

Bunty's Wartime Diary

Author's Note

The following pages contain Bunty's diary – entries in italics – between 1 January and 10 June 1943. I have tried to keep them as close as possible to how she originally wrote them. Beneath some entries are notes I made to hopefully offer some context to what she is describing.

Glennis Amy Leatherdale, 157 Croxted Rd, West Dulwich, SE21 GIP.

Friday, 1 January

Last week of 2nd wk Christmas holiday. Duckmann plaster taken off and Maynard measured for calliper.

Eric and Josey called one afternoon to see Pip who is in bed with rather nasty cough.

Revised physiology in evening and wrote to Tony.

Earlier in day sent off order of books to Churchill Ltd.

Duckmann and Maynard were patients of Bunty's at Guy's Hospital, where she was training in physiotherapy. Pip was her brother Peter, four years older than Bunty.

Saturday, 2 January

On duty in morning – how I loathe going in on Saturdays, makes week-end so short!

Posted Tony's letter – airmail. Spent evening at Nancy's meeting her cousin Caisnie for second time. My approval of him increased and feel myself becoming envious of a certain Betsy. He is a sargent-pilot – flew fighter aircraft during Battle of Britain was later taken prisoner in Algeria but gained his freedom when the British invaded N. Africa. He is blond, moustached and very easy to converse with.

Nancy Campbell was one of Bunty's best friends. Nancy's brother Donald and Bunty's brother Pip were good friends, while Nancy and Bunty went to school together. The pair remained close until Nancy's death from cancer in 1983 at the age of sixty. Bunty was by her side.

Sunday, 3 January

Today has been most pleasant!

In the morning cousin Dick turned up, also I washed my hair.

Josey, Pat and Eric came to tea in the afternoon and we spend an enjoyable hour community singing to Rick's accompaniment. In the evening to Nancy's. Caisnie still there, also Peggy. Started home about 10.felt very pleased about the comparatively early night ahead. Caisnie walked home with me, came in, was besieged with questions from the family and stayed relating his experiences 'til past midnight – early night smashed on head but well worth it!

Dick Leatherdale was a cousin on Bunty's father's side. It seems he was always an entertaining and much-welcomed houseguest.

Monday, 4 January

Back at work feeling very tired. Acquired new patient Collins, fr. fib and tib in Fagge. Duncan back on treatment otherwise things as usual. Home about 6.15. Managed to do a little work – still very tired so retired at 10 – even this is not as early as I'd hoped.

Weather has been icy today and Everdon like an ice-box.

Collins was treated for a fractured fibula and tibia. Duncan was another patient. Fagge was the ward at Guy's Hospital on the south bank of the Thames in Central London where Bunty was training. Everdon was the house at Orpington on the southeast edge of London where Bunty and her fellow physiotherapy students attended lectures.

Tuesday, 5 January

1st p.m.

A very tiring day. Extremely cold weather again, and I didn't get warm until I finally went to bed with a couple of hot water bottles. Everdon is a miserable place at the best of times but in this weather it's impossible.

Wednesday, 6 January

Much warmer today – but has rained unceasingly.

Caught the ten to one train to Charing X. and after a visit to the Leicester Square Fortes I saw 'Squadron Leader X' at the London Pavilion. Eric Portman up to expectations but I prefer him in a more sympathetic role. Met Mummy, Daddy and Cousin Dick who had been to see 'Let's face it' then dinner at Casa Pepe's. Amusing incident re cabilleros and senoras in which Daddy and Dick mistook meaning!

Fortes was a restaurant in Leicester Square, and Casa Pepe's a Spanish eatery in Soho. The amusing incident involved a misunderstanding over which was the gents' toilets.

Squadron Leader X (1943) was a film about a German secret agent (played by Eric Portman) masquerading as a British airman who, after parachuting into Belgium, inadvertently ends up being taken to Britain. The film also starred Ann Dvorak.

Thursday, 7 January

A usual week day. Weather absolutely appalling. it has rained since yesterday morning without stopping. But at least it has been warmer. I worked for a couple of hours in the evening, had a bath and got to bed about 11.30. And as usual I'd decided to have an early night!

Friday, 8 January

It has been dry but intensely cold today, a heavy frost persisting throughout.

Duncan had his stitches taken out this morning and his muscles are still remarkably strong. This shows that all the strengthening up prior to the operation were by no means wasted.

Worked for a bit in the evening and before starting washed my hair.

Thank goodness I'm not on duty tomorrow!

Saturday, 9 January

Went with mother to see 'The Pied Piper' in the afternoon, very good film. Nancy in bed with a cold. Spent the morning in bed. Haven't done this for a long time but it was so cold and I had a bit of a headache and just couldn't get up.

It was a shock on reading the paper to find that Flt/Lt Richard Hillary had been killed. I enjoyed his book 'The Last Enemy' so much that I felt I knew him personally and like him very much. He was only 23, an exceedingly good writer and had been thro' so much already in this war. why couldn't he have lived?

The Pied Piper (1942), starring Monty Woolley, Roddy McDowall and Anne Baxter, follows the plight of an Englishman holidaying in France when the Germans invade, who ends up taking children to safety. Richard Hillary (born 20 April 1919, died 8 January 1943) was a Flight Lieutenant in the Royal Air Force. He suffered serious burns to his face and hands in 1940 after becoming trapped in the burning cockpit of his Supermarine Spitfire when it was shot down over the North Sea. After extensive surgery, he returned to service but crashed on 8 January 1943 during a night time training flight, killing both himself and radio operator Sergeant Wilfred Fison. Details of how he died were not published at the time.

Sunday, 10 January

After a warning headache thro' out yesterday, and a very disturbed night, I awoke to find myself with a roaring cold! Got up because the night had seemed so long and I thought it would be a relief. However, in the afternoon my head was throbbing so much that I thought bed the best place after all. Spent the rest of the day and night wafted between a disturbed sleep and sleepy consciousness. Cannot get Richard Hillary out of my mind. Am rereading his book which seems to have an added power of moving me.

Monday, 11 January

Spent the entire day in bed. My 'blitz' cold began to subside again quite happily. A. Maude arrived in the morning and cousin Dick (who came last night) departed. Shirley Wylde's father called in the evening to pick up the Stanley Holloway poems and the sailor uniform for Jane Hewitt. She needs them for the massage dept entertainment. I cannot truthfully say I shall be disappointed at being unable to see it. Am afraid the possibilities of it being a flop are not small!

Maude was an aunt of Bunty's. Shirley Wylde and Jane Hewitt were acquaintances of Bunty's. The massage department was part of the physiotherapy training centre.

Tuesday, 12 January

Maude stayed here last night but left this morning. Richard Hillary was cremated at Golders Green this morning. There has been nothing in the papers about how he died and as he was not killed in action I am curious to know. How completely broken his parents must be feeling tonight.

I have spent a quiet day still at home but studying a good deal. My cold is still in the sniffly nose stage but throbbing headache has completely vanished. However I shall not go in tomorrow as it is 1/2 day and is not worth it.

Wednesday, 13 January

Nancy popped in for an hour in the evening. Saw Margery while out this afternoon.

Another pleasant lay in this morning – cold has now reached throaty stage – very effective. Went for a walk with mother, the weather was almost like spring-time. Bought a new file from Lydals and ordered two more, and refills.

In afternoon kept appointment at Dr Browns – have lost no weight. Am not surprised after Christmas. He says fatness definitely due to diet, not glands. Am rather relieved about this and have seriously told myself for millionth time to eat less! Had a long walk with Midge in afternoon and ate light dinner. Wonder how long this will last!

Lydals was a stationery shop. The files Bunty bought were paper ones. Midge was a friend of Bunty's who lived with the Leatherdales in West Dulwich. It was common for people to live with others during the war. There were 45 million changes of address between 1939 and 1945 in a population of 30 million.

Thursday, 14 January

Back to work again. Apparently the entertainment which I was so dubious about went off well.

Now there are talks of a dance. I only wish I could work up more enthusiasm over these set affairs – unfortunately!

Still, if Pip is at home then, (Feb 13 provisionally), and comes with me I shan't mind.

I managed to carry out my non fat-eating campaign today quite successfully. Oh please let me have enough will to really get results this time!

Our 3 monthly exams come off next Tuesday and Wednesday – daren't think about them!

Friday, 15 January

Work went quite happily today – Duncan and Ridgway were off treatment so I did 'auntie' for Shirley. Everybody is getting in an awful panic about the exams – definitely including myself – I don't seem to know where to start revision.

Kept to diet quite well again today, but had one or two bad moments, one Cornish pasty at lunchtime and ginger cake in the evening. Oh! to be the streamline type!!

Washed my hair before retiring about 11.15.

Saturday, 16 January

On duty this morning – caught 11.55 back home and learned on arrival there that a Canadian had phoned up giving his name as Leatherdale. Apparently he had seen our name in the phone directory and wondered if we were any relation. Daddy has asked him to come to tea tomorrow. We have no idea what to expect. He's probably a tough soldier, fortyish, with a wife and kids at home!! Anyway, tomorrow we'll know.

Couple of hours work in afternoon and supper with Nancy in evening. Am afraid my diet gets rather lax at weekends!

Sunday, 17 January

Am writing this in bed about 11.30 before retiring after a most eventful day.

Put in some anatomy revision in the morning. Dick (cousin), A. Eva, Uncle and Janet turned up and we all awaited with bated breath our Canadian. He arrived, a young sergeant observer in R.C.A.F, very pleasant, quiet of manner and rather overcome by the crowd of us strangers!

He is stationed at Bournemouth at present – returns there tomorrow.

Just as we were sitting down to supper the sirens went. Planes were over soon after and the ack-ack barrage was very heavy. We heard three bombs drop – that is three we were certain of – may have been more.

It was just like old times and I can't say I enjoyed it. Hope we see some more of Grant, like him.

Grant was shot down three weeks after visiting the Leatherdales in London.

The following day's *Evening Standard* reported on the raids that disturbed the supper. Between twenty-five and thirty enemy aircraft came between 8.00 pm and 10.00 pm, but many did not reach London: 'industrial damage was slight'. An AA (anti-aircraft) shell fell in Lincoln Road, Enfield, and exploded, injuring four people, one a warden. All were taken to hospital. The *Standard* reported:

> Mrs Sartin and Mrs Stockdale were killed when a bomb completely demolished four semi-detached houses. Three of Mrs Stockdale's children – a boy and two girls – were injured but are making good progress in hospital.
>
> In Whiteley Road, Gipsy Hill, a sailor who was home on leave was seriously injured when an anti-aircraft shell fell in the roadway. An anti-aircraft shell fell in the doorway of a house in Alexandra Drive, Gipsy Hill, killing Mr J. Ravenal and a woman not yet identified.
>
> An AA shell fell through the roof of the men's ward at Redhill hospital Edgware but did not explode. No one was injured.

The paper also reported an AA shell falling in the garden of Buckingham Palace, destroying a plot of Brussels sprouts. Many shops and houses were also damaged. A firewatcher, George Parker, and a woman who was running along the street, were killed. Another firewatcher, caretaker Robert Moore, 50, was killed and three others seriously injured when an AA shell crashed through the wall protecting an air raid shelter in a block of flats in Tessaly Road Battersea. Frederick Charles Simmons of Bickersteth Road and Harry Millard of Derinton Road, both of Tooting, were killed by a shell. Lydia Hele, Marlborough Road, Collier's Wood, was killed when flak pierced the window of her home, and a PC Burns, 48, of Chelsea police station, died while staying with a friend in Bromley when struck by a fragment of AA shell in the street.

A special constable called Jelf was seriously injured when an AA shell exploded in the road opposite a police box in Court Road, Orpington, but 400 dancers at a Home Guard party in a hall in the outer area of London escaped when three bombs fell close by.

'Windows were blown in and the dancers were showered with broken glass. A gas main took fire but the flames were quickly put out', the paper reported. Some damage was also done to a London cricket ground.

Monday, 18 January

Another raid early this morning about 4.45–6.45. Learned later that ten planes had been brought down during night. Our bombers raided Berlin again during the night so we are expecting another tonight.

We lost 22 aircraft last night – doesn't do thinking about!

This afternoon we had Pathology and theory three monthly test.

Papers were really very easy but I'm afraid I muffed them.

Sirens went this evening about 7.30 but it seemed to be a false alarm – up 'til now 11 pm. We've had no raid but the night is young yet!

According to *Evening Standard* air-reporter James Stuart, sixty German bombers crossed the English coast, headed for London in the two raids on Sunday night and early Monday morning.

Ten were destroyed. The raids involved a mixture of Junkers 88s, Heinkel 111s and Dornier 217s, which flew in over south and southeast England. Some took part in both raids. Stuart wrote:

The objective of all the planes was London. But the outer defences operated with just the same deadly affect as the guns in London. The fact that many bombs were dropped on many places in South and South East England suggests that many of the raiders were turned back by the barrage. It is certain that, faced with such a barrage as the raiders, many of them that did return will be out of commission for some little time.

The German News Agency said that the early morning raid saw the 'strong forces of the German Luftwaffe' attack London with thousands of high-explosive and incendiary bombs dropped, particularly over the area southwest of the Great Thames loop, causing 'considerable damage'.

They said two German planes failed to return, with six overall failing to make it from both raids.

The *Standard* also said a simultaneous raid was carried out on Berlin, with twenty-two British bombers missing. The ten missing German bombers represented a 'much higher percentage by our defences than the loss of twenty-two of our aircraft in the Berlin Raid', reported the paper.

The destruction of four of the ten downed German craft was attributed to Wing Commander C.M. Wight-Boycott, 32-year-old leader of the Beaufighter Squadron of Fighter Command, a new night-fighting record.

A squadron member told the *Standard*: 'The enemy aircraft were jinking all over the sky in attempts to evade us. They were obviously jittery before they even knew we were there.'

The raids killed six people, with houses also damaged. The *Standard* commented: 'London's barrage was the fiercest and most spectacular ever. Never before have all the A.A. (anti-aircraft) devices and tactics been used.'

One problem highlighted by the *Evening Standard* was that of 'troublesome rubbernecks' who went out into the streets to see the raids. Sir Wyndham Deedes, chief air-raid warden of Bethnal Green, said:

> The public showed a great deal of stupid negligence. They stood about in the open from sheer curiosity. People who wander around the streets during Ack-Ack gunfire are helping Hitler by offering themselves as voluntary casualties.

He also said there were far too many young children still in London. One other incident of note during the raid, involved a man who held up the Shanghai Restaurant on Greek Street in Soho, with what appeared to be a revolver. He took £9 10s in notes from the cash register before escaping.

Tuesday, 19 January

No raid last night much to everyone's surprise!

Anatomy and physiology paper this afternoon which, like yesterday's, was not really difficult but fear I haven't answered very well.

I'd finished about half an hour too soon which looks rather as if my answers were too brief – however we shall see.

Glorified in a completely lazy evening doing no work after swatting in panic for the last fortnight.

Began to scheme in my head about giving a party round about Feb 2nd. There are one or two big problems, lack of boys and difficulty on transport however I shall see how the folks react to the idea!

Wednesday, 20 January

Nancy came down in evening during which time sirens sounded. Nothing developed.

Caught the 11.55 home to-day by getting Glenys W to sign off for me. Had been home about 5 mins when sirens sounded. Quite a few planes about and considerable gun-fire.

The balloon in the Polytechnic grounds was shot down and made an awful row which for a moment I mistook for a bomb.

Learned later that about thirty fighter bombers had tried to get thro' to London but only six succeeded.

Thirty small children were killed when a school was hit and Surrey Docks were set on fire.

Went for a long walk in afternoon I think I saw Duggie Marsh. However he had gone by before I could be certain. Have written to him tonight in case he thought I was just being snotty.

The *London Evening Standard* carried one line about the school being hit, although much more was to be written about it in the following days and weeks. The paper on Wednesday, 20 January, reported German raiders dive-bombing a heavily populated area of London, machine gunning a railway station and a high street from just forty feet above the rooftops.

The street was practically empty as most people had run for cover upon hearing the engines, but one man who was riding a bike was hit, said an article on the *Standard's* front page.

Two men, a mother and child were killed in South East London. The paper's air reporter, James Stuart, said forty fighter bombers, carrying small bombs, set out for London, but only ten got through the British defences. Calling it 'probably the biggest raid since the Battle of Britain', Stuart wrote:

Bunty was born in 1924, the daughter of Alfred and Gertrude Leatherdale and sister of Peter.
(Courtesy of the Leatherdale family)

Bunty as a young girl with her nurse.
(Courtesy of the Leatherdale family)

Being a baker and therefore in a reserved occupation, Bunty's father Alfred did not need to fight in the First World War but he chose to sign up. He was wounded in the Battle of the Somme by a piece of shrapnel in his hand.
(Courtesy of the Leatherdale family)

Pauline, Peter, Shirley, Gertie, Alf, Amy & Bunt

Bunty (far right) is pictured on a seaside holiday in 1934 with her cousins, parents and aunt Amy.
(Courtesy of the Leatherdale family)

The Leatherdales moved into 157 Croxted Road in West Dulwich shortly after Bunty's birth.
(Courtesy of the Leatherdale family)

Bunty began keeping her diary at the start of 1943 when she was an eighteen-year-old trainee physiotherapist.
(Courtesy of the Leatherdale family)

Bunty (right) would often go on cycling rides with her best friends Peggy (left) and Nancy (centre) in the countryside around London. Bicycles were hard to come by but, being a baker, Bunty's father Alfred had good connections with other trades and managed to source some for his daughter and her friends. (Courtesy of the Leatherdale family)

Bunty's friend Nancy lived at Haddon Lodge, Bunty would often visit her there.
(Courtesy of the Leatherdale family)

Alfred Leatherdale grew vegetables and housed chickens – known as his Little Ladies – in the family's garden. (*Courtesy of the Leatherdale family*)

Bunty's brother Pip became an engineer in the RAF during the war. He is pictured here in the back garden of the family home with his girlfriend Pat, nicknamed 'Paddles' by Bunty. (*Courtesy of the Leatherdale family*)

everyone's buying the new
handy size Hovis
it's so economical
Baked daily by
A. Leatherdale
Head Office: 32 KENNINGTON LANE
TELEPHONE: RELIANCE 1951 & 1383

The Leatherdale Bakery was started by Bunty's grandfather and at its peak it had twelve shops around London and provided bread for Harrods. (*Courtesy of the Leatherdale family*)

Nancy was one of Bunty's best friends. (*Courtesy of the Leatherdale family*)

Alfred and Gertrude stayed in London throughout the war. They had wanted their daughter Bunty to be evacuated, possibly to New Zealand, but she refused to go so stayed with them.
(Courtesy of the Leatherdale family)

Bunty's brother Peter was four years older than her and worked as an engineer for the RAF during the war. Note the cover over the headlight of his motorbike, a condition of the blackout.
(Courtesy of the Leatherdale family)

During the time of Bunty's diary, her brother Peter was courting Pat, but he went onto marry Betty, with the pair going on to have three children. Peter and Betty are pictured here on their wedding day with Peter's best man Bob Adams and Bunty.
(Courtesy of the Leatherdale family)

After the war Bunty met and married a Lancaster navigator called Frank Leatherdale. They divorced a few years later after having two sons together.
(Courtesy of the Leatherdale family)

Here they are pictured on their wedding day with both sets of parents.
(Courtesy of the Leatherdale family)

Bunty's mother died in 1951. Following her death, Bunty would accompany her father to various dinners and dances, here they are together at one such event in 1954. (Courtesy of the Leatherdale family)

Bunty was close friends with Nancy until her death from cancer at the age of sixty in 1983. Bunty was by her side when Nancy died. (Courtesy of the Leatherdale family)

At the time of writing, Bunty's family consisted of two sons, three grandsons, several daughters-in-law and two great grandson's (and a great grand-dog). She has been living happily in Bradford-on-Avon for some thirty years. (Courtesy of the Leatherdale family)

The raiders seemed to have attacked in three formations on the South East, from the Thames Estuary and from the Isle of Wight. Most of them were intercepted and were broken up before they reached London hence the scattered bombing of more than ten districts. The raiders were fighter bombers carrying small bombs. Both the Messerschmitt and the F.W. 90 take two 250-pounders.

The weather was cloudy in the Straits of Dover and this helped the raiders. It certainly looks as though the Luftwaffe have taken up the challenge of the RAF. Nothing would be more welcomed so far as our pilots are concerned but the Germans will always be able to surprise the defence in cloudy weather.

Thursday, 21 January

The sirens went again last night after I'd written the day's entry in here. It postponed my going to bed for about an hour making it somewhere around midnight – sirens disturbed me again at ten past one so, not unnaturally, I've been dead all day.

The number killed when that school was hit yesterday has gone up to 45. How ghastly it is!

I am making a gallant effort to get to bed early to-night. It is only 9.30 and I'm on my way!

Received airgraph from Tony, in much the same strain as previous letters.

Airgraph was the postal service during the war.

The bomb strike on Sandhurst Road School in Catford sparked national outrage. According to Lewisham War Memorial researchers, a 500 kg bomb struck a direct hit on the four-storey school at lunchtime. Many children were eating their lunch in the school's dinner hall and it was here where most of the casualties were – twenty-four pupils and two teachers killed. Five more died on the school's main staircase and nine were killed on the second floor. Three teachers were killed in the staff room and another in the school's science room. In total, forty-four people lost their lives.

The *London Evening Standard* of Thursday, 21 January carried harrowing accounts of families searching through rubble to find their missing children. The paper notes that the death toll could have been much worse – many of the children had fortunately gone home for their lunch.

Rescuers did speak of the bravery of one girl, 12-year-old Molly Kinnerman, who was found with her legs pinned down by a piece of timber. Mr E.W. Palmer, a plumber, said, 'I clambered over the debris and heard her say "don't leave me". Both her legs were fractured, she did not whimper.'

Three other girls buried with Molly were recovered alive. The paper also carried a picture of 6-year-old Shirley Borman who was rescued from the debris. She would normally have gone home for lunch, but the day of the raid was the first time she had stayed at school to eat.

On Friday, 22 January, the final death toll stood at forty-four. A mass funeral for all the victims was to be held the following Wednesday.

The funeral of thirty-one of the thirty-nine children and five teachers was held on Wednesday, 27 January. The bodies were buried in a fifty-feet-long grave, lined with boughs of laurel and fir. Around 7,000 mourners attended.

Friday, 22 January

Usual working day. Great deal of air activity Orpington way all day. Learned in the evening that daylight bombing raids had been carried out over Germany.

Plans rushing ahead for dance at Everdon on Feb 13 – I've been allotted 'decorations' with Glenys Walwork. They want hearts and cupids etc to stick round walls as it'll be St Valentine's Eve.

Midge has gone home for the week-end so household consists of just the family, rather a pleasant change.

Washed my hair before retiring.

Saturday, 23 January

Have spent a very happy day this morning. had breakfast in bed, then to Streatham to purchase shoes and stockings. Was unsuccessful in my quest so took bus to Piccadilly Circus. Here, at Dolcis, I bought a very pleasing pair of shoes in natural pigskin.

Met mummy and we lunched at Casa Pepe.

Decided to go to flics, but on passing the Globe Theatre changed our minds and saw Owen Nares, Constance Cummings in 'The Petrified Forest'.

Good entertainment. Then to tea at Trocadero – also very pleasant. Met Jean and Ronny coming home and they popped in for a short time. Spent rest of evening happily at home with mummy and daddy.

Dolcis was a shoe shop in Piccadilly Circus, Casa Pepe a restaurant in the same area, and the Trocadero an eatery in central London.

Sunday, 24 January

Supper at Nancy's, Midge came back in the evening.

A usual enjoyable Sunday morning – got up late and just pottered around doing odd jobs until dinner time. In the afternoon Nancy and I walked to Streatham Hill Theatre where a charity event was being held.

Personally, Michael Redgrave was the attraction and even if the rest of the show had been rotten (which it certainly wasn't) it would have been well worth it. He sang three old Norfolk songs very charmingly and as usual his appearance and personality stole my heart away!!

Michael Redgrave, who was knighted in 1959, was an English actor born in Bristol in 1908, the son of a silent-movie star and actress. He joined the Royal Navy in 1941, but was dismissed a year later on medical grounds, so he returned to the stage. His film credits included the 1955 film *The Dam Busters*, the story of the British bombers targeting German dams. He died in 1985.

Monday, 25 January

A moderately pleasant Monday. I acquired a new patient, Mrs Read with a fractured femur. I might say I'm getting a bit fed up with this particular injury having three on my list at present.

Duncan's leg is at last picking up again. Mrs Cameron gave us a lecture in the afternoon on the amount of study we are expected 'to get there'!

Left me very depressed! Received letter from Gordon which didn't cheer me as much as usual.

Tuesday, 26 January

Mr Kingshott went home today amidst fervent farewells and many smiles. Poor Mr Duckmann felt very envious I believe, but still, I don't think it'll be long now before his turn comes.

Caught 20 min earlier train coming home at cost of running to station, with my blouse (discarded for massage) in my hand and my blazer tightly drawn, remind me to maintain respectability.

Nancy popped down in the evening and when she left Daddy asked me what I'd like to do next Wednesday week to celebrate my birthday. Decided on theatre and dinner with a party of 8 – hope this works out.

Wednesday, 27 January

On going to treat Maynard found that the previous evening he was up, and his crutch slipped – he fell fracturing his femur – really – of all the bad luck!

Caught five to one train home and kept appointment with Mr Williams at four. He started to restop one of my teeth but the gum began to bleed and he left it, booking me at 11.30 next Sunday to finish the job. Stayed and had tea with Mrs Williams and Pat.

In the evening I did but a very little work – wrote to Gordon and the Polyfoto Studio about his photos – then to bed at 10 o clock – one of the earliest nights we had for a long time. Terminating another pleasant mid-week break.

Mr Williams was a family friend and Bunty's dentist. His daughter, Pat Williams, was the girlfriend of Peter 'Pip' Leatherdale, Bunty's brother.

The Polyfoto studio was the 1940s equivalent of a passport photo booth today.

Thursday, 28 January

Uneventful morning. Heard our exam results in the afternoon; to my colossal surprise I came second in the anatomy and phys. paper and fourth in the path. and theory paper. In spite of these high placings my marks were nothing to be proud of – 49/80 for first paper and 50/80 for second, which just shows how low the standard of our set is at present. However, it's a great relief to know I'm not the worst.

Duncan is going on leave for ten days from tomorrow and so, with Maynard off treatment, work looks like slacking off.

Friday, 29 January

Mr Duckmann informs me he is going home shortly. He has certainly made an excellent recovery. Today has been uneventful. Started my weekend question in the evening but Nancy's arrival stopped it rather abruptly – this doesn't mean that it (Nancy's arrival) wasn't very welcome. She told me how Peggy had misconstrued 'Arsenic and Old Lace' – the play we are going to next Wednesday.

Mother has a rather tiresome cold which forced her to bed early in the evening. I washed my hair.

Nancy and Peggy were two of Bunty's closest friends.

Saturday, 30 January

On duty this morning. Treated a frightful man named Toze. Definitely the worst patient I've come across. Thank God it's only for today. Lunched in Bromley and from there to shorthand, for tea with cousin Doris and Ken. This was very pleasant, and I thoroughly enjoyed my afternoon with them.

Arrived home to find Cousin Dick had got a weekend pass and was naturally spending it with us.

What a pity more of my relatives aren't as easy to get on with as Dick! Returned in a happy state of mind.

Sunday, 31 January

Mr Williams phoned this morning to suggest that I left my 'tooth' appointment 'til next Sunday as the weather was so wet and wild.

I agreed strongly with the suggestion. Nancy's to tea – Donald Goldie and Harry Dudgeon there also. A good time was had by all!

Diana and Jill paid a surprise visit later in the evening – first to our house, then onto Campbells. On reaching home I found that Duggie Marsh had phoned earlier. He is going to phone again during the week. It'll be rather pleasant hearing from him again, at least, I hope so!

Monday, 1 February

On this, the last day of my eighteenth year, Peter's papers came calling him to the RAF. Please God, may he have as much good fortune as was bestowed on him in the previous period.

Looking back upon the year I can see that it hasn't been nearly such fun as my seventeenth year was. That year when Tony and Gordon and Donald made such happy memories.

They are all abroad now, may the best of luck be with them also.

The bright spot in the last year was undoubtedly my switching from banking to physio-therapy. However much I curse the hard work there is no job I'd rather be doing at present.

Pip seems very happy at the prospect of returning to the RAF. His past months in the civilian job have been a great strain on his mental peace – in fact, he has had little.

Before commencing with physiotherapy training in 1942, a profession which ended up being her career until retirement, Bunty worked in banking.

Peter was an engineer in the RAF, but when not in service, he worked for the family business, the bakery.

Tuesday, 2 February

On arriving home after a rather more taxing day than usual it was my delightful job to unravel various parcels and read various cards. All the usual excitement of a birthday flooded in and I felt extremely happy.

I had some wonderful presents from Daddy, an exquisite gold chain bracelet – Mummy a gold Guys broach and longed for 'petit point' bag – and from Pip a super Dunhill lighter. All my other gifts were of excellent choice but those were the top numbers!!

As we are all going out tomorrow I decided to wash my hair knowing how the result adds greatly to the feeling of looking my best and consequent enjoyment.

Wrote to Donald Chalmers inviting him to our dance on the 13th Feb.

Bunty still has and treasures the gold chain bracelet. It is filled with charms she has acquired over the years. During the war years, she said it was her lucky token:

'My charm bracelet had to come down to the cellar with me every time there was air raid, even if the air raid had started I would go and get it, I was so superstitious. I also wore it under my tunic in exams.'

Wednesday, 3 February

Caught the early train home. I kept appointment with Mr Williams at 2.30. Met Nancy, Peggy, Pip, Pat and Daddy at Strand Theatre in the evening. With Mummy and Midge this made the party eight. The play 'Arsenic and Old Lace' was great fun – after trying the Piccadilly Hotel for dinner, but being unsuccessful we managed to get in Oddernino's. Although the meal was very good I didn't enjoy it enormously – there seems to be a jinx on that place because the same thing happened at Pat's 21st. I should have enjoyed it but I just didn't quite inexplicable – but nevertheless – true.

Thursday, 4 February

Felt considerably brighter on getting up than I'd expected after my late night. This energy was maintained until lectures started, then oh boy! What I'd have given for a bed. Luckily Wareham was away and we finished at 3.30. I slept going home in the train and then flopped into a chair to sleep a bit more. Worked for a couple of hours after dinner and was in bed by ten.

The war news continues to be good. Russian victories mounting and German communiques getting more and more un-German!

Truda Wareham was one of Bunty's physiotherapy tutors.

Friday, 5 February

Spent the evening at Nancy's after a normal working day.

Saturday, 6 February

In the morning I spent a couple of hours in the town with mother 'frock-hunting'. This proved unsuccessful. We cheered ourselves up over an excellent lunch at the Criterion. In the evening Midge took me to the ballet (Sadlers Wells) as a birthday present. We saw Copalia [Coppélia] which was, of course, perfect.

After the show had the novel experience of going backstage, Midge visiting a former colleague of hers, Celia Franca. The 'dressing-room' and atmosphere was completely as one would expect with its hard, bright lights and untidiness. Passed Robert Helpmann when leaving, much to our delight.

Robert Helpmann was an Australian dancer and actor, born in 1909. He died in 1986.

One of his most famous roles was that of the terrifying Child-Catcher in the 1968 musical film Chitty Chitty Bang Bang, adapted from an Ian Fleming novel by Roald Dahl.

Sunday, 7 February

Spent a marvellous day with Nancy and Peggy cycling in Surrey. We took the train to Dorking and finished up near Guildford after travelling by a most irregular route. Two Canadian soldiers also spending their afternoon cycling aimlessly around the countryside joined us and guided us to a pleasant guest-house where we enjoyed a delicious tea and much joking and laughing. Learnt that soldiers were called Bill Ryan and Archie, the former being my favourite.

When we left them we passed thro' Sheer and found time to visit the Silent Pools which are really beautiful. Calm clear waters of unimaginable colours.

Monday, 8 February

Awoke quite cheerfully but developed a stomach ache and sickness as day progressed. Think it must be something to do with tongue sandwiches I had yesterday. It looked suspiciously blue. By the evening felt really bad and had to cancel visit to Nancy's which I was very sorry about as it was her 20th birthday. Was violently sick and hurried to bed with a sickening headache.

Tuesday, 9 February

Spent morning in bed, my stomach still behaving badly. Got up at midday and wrote letters and generally pottered around until Mummy and Daddy came back from 'The Dearest Sons' where Pip had taken them.

Nancy came down in the evening and I wished her an overdue 'many happy returns'. Mr and Mrs Kennett, Reg and Gladys also called, and bored me so much. I thought I'd scream. I've never met a family who have such a sedative effect on me! Have written to Bill Ryan. Bet I live to regret it!

Wednesday, 10 February

Didn't go in this morning – neither did Midge 'cause of a cold. With Pip that made three of us at home, quite a crowd for a week day. Glenys Walwark and

Eleanor Hodgkins came to lunch and we set to in the afternoon cutting hearts out of paper – decorations for the dance at Everdon. G and E are two of the nicest girls in the set, in my opinion, I might even say the nicest!

In the evening Bert Higgins came to collect Len's cake – he is 21 on Friday. As the icing was smudged Daddy is going to have it redone and I'm to take it on Saturday morning. Len is in the R.A.F. now and I rather hope I renew his acquaintance. What I remember of him is quite promising.

Thursday, 11 February

Was in very good spirits all day today. My bilious attack must have done me good. Back at the hospital to find that Duncan had returned from his leave and been discharged since I'd been away. Disappointed at not seeing him again, he was a nice lad. Continued heart-snipping out in the evening. Nancy and Pat popped in during the evening, Nancy informing me that her cousin, Cairnie, is getting married shortly. Lucky Betsy!

Finished one string of hearts and am rather pleased with result. Am wondering how Glenys and Eleanor are progressing with theirs.

Friday, 12 February

Following a normal Friday I set to in the evening to finish the decorations for Everdon. Completed another string of hearts and produced a few cupids and faces to stick on the walls. Am beginning at last to look forward to the dance. Started preparing for bed about ten but after bathing and washing my hair in the last scraps of Evan Williams shampoo (saved for the occasion), the hour was fairly late. Midge away for the night following Andy Davis party.

Shampoo was rationed from 1942. Women would often wash their hair in washing powder or just water. To add shine, brunettes would sometimes rinse their hair in vinegar or beer, while blondes would use lemon juice. Vegetable dyes like henna or rhubarb would be used to create colourful cuts.

Saturday, 13 February

Had breakfast with Mummy and Daddy – a rare thing for Sat. morning. Set out for Mrs Higgins with Len's 21st cake and pastries etc. After considerable difficulty I found the place – they having moved from the address I'd been given. Len had not altered much – really quite a pleasant lad. By the time I got to Everdon it was lunchtime but I joined in with the decorations and we'd finished by about three. Went home, rested and changed then set forth to Everdon again with Pip.

The dance was a great success, I personally thoroughly enjoyed it. I felt that I looked my best, which, of course goes a long way.

Sunday, 14 February

With pleasant memories of last night still vivid I started another happy day about 10. It was Pip's last Sunday at home for some time and we had quite a crowd for tea. Mr and Mrs Sheffield, Pat, Nancy, Cousin Dick, Shirley W and Monty Riddle whom I had heard so much about. He reminded Nancy and I strongly of Charles Laughton and seemed quite an amusing sought of person.

Anna also turned up. It is months since we've seen her and her playing made me reminiscent of the days when Gordon and Dudley were at home. What a joy it is to watch and hear her play!

Monday, 15 February

At lunchtime I changed three book tokens at Smiths, buying Quentin Reynolds 'Only the stars are Neutral' and 'Signed with their honour' by James Aldridge. Miss Stephens being away resulted in our leaving Everdon one period early much to our delight. I don't think any of us are conscientious enough to regret the missing lecture!

Pat came round for the evening and I did but a little work on the strength of Pip returning to R.A.F. tomorrow. The evening was spent happily with everyone in good humour.

Gwen Vernon popped in later on to add her au revoirs.

Tuesday, 16 February

Went to the B.R. for lunch with Moira Simpson, Pam Herbertson, Hester Wilkes and Shirley. It was really a very pleasant change and I had an excellent meal for it. There is a truly communal atmosphere about these places which is rather nice.

Unfortunately, either the meal or a not particularly early night previously resulted in my nearly falling asleep in the Theory lecture – I fear it was the lunch and it is because of this that I don't make a habit of a hot midday meal.

Did my weekend question – very overdue – in the evening.

The BR was the British Restaurant, one of 2,160 communal kitchens set up in 1940 to feed people, without the need for ration vouchers. They were initially called the Community Feeding Centres but the name was changed by Winston Churchill. The maximum price for a meal was 9d – equivalent to £1.24 in 2015. Private restaurants also weren't subject to rations, but they were restricted. No meal could be more than three courses and the maximum price was five shillings – £6.20 in 2015.

Wednesday, 17 February

Left the hospital early because Mr Smith was off treatment and was then able to catch 11.55 train. Enjoyed a most appetising lunch with mother (Midge didn't come home) and lounged, read, and dappled in some work during afternoon.

In the evening went with Nancy and Diana to the flics. Diana was just up for 24 hrs being stationed at Epping, I think.

We saw 'Mr Washington Slept Here' with Jack Benny. It was great fun and I laughed a good deal even tho' t'was the second time I'd seen it.

The film was actually called *George Washington Slept here*. It was released in 1942 and starred Jack Benny and Ann Sheridan, as well as Hattie McDaniel who, in 1939, became the first black African-American to win an Oscar for her role in *Gone With The Wind*.

Thursday, 18 February

The day passed uneventfully. Auntie Blanche was at home when I arrived in the evening but I didn't see much of her as I just got in some quite useful time on leg M.M. I may be wrong but I seem to be finding them easier than the arm ones.

Was very tired so made a real effort and was in bed by 10.15.

Daddy had a letter from Pip. He appears to be liking it at Thornley Island which is unusual in such a short time.

Friday, 19 February

The weather has been glorious today. We had our lunch and an exercise class in the garden at Everdon. I hope we do this a lot in the summer.

I finished 'Only the stars are neutral' today and have thoroughly enjoyed reading it. Quentin Reynolds seems a likeable man and his writing held my interest all the time.

Life as a foreign correspondent on a paper must be grand if one has the ability.

I am now going to see to the old hot water bottle and then wash my hair – yippee! Tomorrow is Saturday and I've wangled another one off.

Quentin Reynolds was an American war correspondent for *Collier's Weekly*, and author of more than two dozen books.

Saturday, 20 February

Received a letter from Bill Ryan! Bought picture by Peter Scott.

Went with mother to Pratt's in the morning to look at a fur coat she likes. It's really a lovely one – dyed squirrel – and if she decides to have it she'll let me have her pony skin one.

In the afternoon I went to an old girl's meeting at Streatham Hill. It was very disappointing because there were none of my contemporaries there. Afterwards I met Nancy and Peggy in Croydon and paid yet another visit to the Anglo Polish ballet. They are carrying on gallantly in spite of Konarski and Halama's desertion – but are not nearly so good.

The Anglo–Polish Ballet was formed in London in 1940 by two dancers, Czeslow Konarski and Alicja Halama.

Sunday, 21 February

Cousin Dick arrived soon after breakfast. He seems to be as good as Pip was at getting off every weekend. Of course he is fairly near – at Horley.

Spent the afternoon and evening at Nancy's – Harry D, Donald G. and Margery also there. I had a grim fit of depression hanging over me which I couldn't shake. Margery was rather irritating and I was not sorry to get home.

When I did I found that Pip had arrived about half an hour early. He is just up for tonight and tomorrow. The camp is definitely the best one he has ever been at. Very efficiently run etc.

Monday, 22 February

Nancy called in the evening. Started treating a new patient – Reavey. He is 19 and seems a pleasant lad. His notes say he attempted suicide and has bad fits of depression, few interests and generally lethargic. I have not found him so and think him quite an interesting patient.

Leaving exercises last period resulted in me missing the 5.40   even so I saw Pip for a few minutes before he left.

It has been beautiful weather today, more like May than February – I hope it continues, fine weather being so cheery. N.B. Ordered records in Orpington.

Tuesday, 23 February

Lunched at the British Restaurant with Moira and Pam.

Altho' I enjoy having lunch there I feel that two main meals a day are too much. Anyway, it's a pleasant occasional change.

Got to Everdon to find that we were having a Path test. Rather a shock, particularly as I'd no notes to refer to with me.

I should think I answered the questions pretty badly which I suppose should not have been the case as we had time to look them up.

Caught 5.20 train home and rejoiced in tomorrow being Wednesday!!

Wednesday, 24 February

Caught the early train home. It was such a lovely early spring day that I got off the train at Sydenham Hill and walked from there.

Enjoyed a leisurely lunch with mother and a similar afternoon telling myself that I'd do some work in the evening with Midge.

My plans were, however, unexpectedly changed when Pat Williams phoned to ask me to go to the 'Regal' with her.

This I did, more to avoid further friction than because I wished to go. However the flic – Pride of the Yankees – was diverting and pleasant and I was finally glad I'd gone.

The 1942 film *Pride of the Yankees* was a biopic of Lou Gehrig, starring Gary Cooper.

Gehrig died in 1941 at the age of 37 from amyotrophic lateral sclerosis (ALS), a debilitating deteriorating condition that was renamed Gehrig's disease. In the sixteen years he played for the Major League baseball side the New York Yankees, Gehrig, who was also a teammate of Babe Ruth, hit 493 home runs. He was diagnosed while still playing. The Yankees retired his number four shirt in his honour.

Thursday, 25 February

Lunched at the B.R. today because mummy and daddy went to Brighton and my evening meal was uncertain. Arrived home to find pools of blood all over the carpet in the dining room. It is from Chum but we don't know quite what's the cause.

Midge very gallantly cleaned it up. I'm afraid I'm not much good at coping with such things.

I washed my hair early in the evening finishing soon after mummy and daddy came home.

They had a very pleasant day altho' mother was disappointed she couldn't see more of the sea – defence measures make this so.

Chum was the family's pet dog.

Friday, 26 February

Had been looking forward to trek to the Shanghai in the evening with Nancy, Margery and Peggy and was very disappointed to learn, when I got home, that Nancy had a cold and arrangements were cancelled. Margery felt similarly dejected so we joined forces and went to the Plaza. Bob Hope in The Ghost Breakers proved an excellent tonic.

After the flic we tried at least six places to get something to eat but were unsuccessful. But we were no longer depressed and caught a train home in good spirits. I'm afraid Margery still irritates me rather!

The Ghost Breakers was a 1940 comedy starring Bob Hope and Paulette Goddard, about their exploits in a haunted castle on a small island close to Cuba.

Saturday, 27 February

Was on duty in the morning and to my surprise rather enjoyed it. Patients were pleasant and everything went smoothly.

After lunch mother and I made a sudden decision to go up to town. Tried for tea at the Troc without success but managed to get a cup at the Empire Leicester Square while waiting for programme to start. We saw Random Harvest which was most entertaining.

Had a fine dinner afterwards at the Cafe de L'Europe and arrived home very pleased with a surprise excursion.

Feel rather ashamed about 3 pictures in a week.

Random Harvest was a 1942 film based on the book of the same name by James Hilton, released the previous year. It was nominated for seven Academy Awards, including for Best Lead Actor for Ronald Colman, who played a shell-shocked, amnesiac First World War veteran.

Sunday, 28 February

Cousin Dick turned up in the morning. In the afternoon met Peggy, Margery, Barbara M, Jean Gayford and Mary Power outside the Garrick where we were going to see a ballet in aid of the VACF.

Nancy was actually sponsor of the party but being in bed left us to go on our own. Ballet, when not performed well, is highly amusing – so we found this performance.

Arrived home to find Partridges from Norwood there.

We were entertained by Dick for about an hour then I popped round to see how Nancy was – she was in excellent spirits. Apparently her American 'Texas Dan' looked them up on Friday evening.

Monday, 1 March

Pip came home in the evening. This put an early stop to my work which I rather regretted as I have an anatomy test on Thursday – altho' I guess I really enjoyed the excuse!

Pip still likes the place but was depressed because two rather unpleasant accidents had occurred.

Some of his fellow ground staff had been killed in an air crash. Also a plane had set fire one night whilst bombing up – the bombs had exploded and shaken everyone up a bit.

Peter was an engineer stationed at Heston aerodrome on the western edge of London.

Prime Minister Neville Chamberlain flew from Heston to Germany three times in two weeks in 1938 to meet Adolf Hitler, the last of which yielding his famous 'peace for our time' speech.

Before the war Heston, which opened in 1929, was also the site of several flight-record attempts and high-profile flying events. In 1939 it became home to the RAF's clandestine photography departments and interceptor units. It was also temporarily used by RAF Polish fighter squadrons flying Spitfires and Hurricanes. Heston officially closed in 1947 as the development of Heathrow nearby rendered flight almost impossible from there. Part of the site now houses Heston Service Station on the M4 motorway.

Tuesday, 2 March

Pat came to dinner and as Pip didn't leave until about eight again I did only a little work. I gaily tell myself I'll do it tomorrow, bet something crops up then and I regret it.

Spent a pleasant couple of hours before Pip went just the family and Pat, with all of us in happy, friendly moods.

Pip certainly seems miles better, mentally and physically, since he was at Heston.

He expects to come up again for a night next week.

Wednesday, 3 March

Much to my annoyance I had to catch the five to one train. This entails so much hanging about and waste of time. On the other hand the 11.55 means such a rush.

Really got down to some work on muscles in the afternoon and early evening.

Bathed and just got installed in the dining room when the sirens went.

It was a short, noisy raid and we retired to the cellar. Midge and I tested each other's anatomy.

This raid was generally expected as the R.A.F. made a very heavy raid over Berlin the other night.

Thursday, 4 March

Another lovely spring day, we really are having a period of perfect weather – the blossom everywhere looking heavenly.

Had lunch in the garden at Everdon and did some last minute swotting for the test.

It proved not to be very difficult and I quite enjoyed doing it.

Friday, 5 March

Shirley was not in today because she has gone to Bala for the weekend. The weather is continuing fine and her weekend will be most enjoyable.

Only had one period in the afternoon – this came as a very pleasant surprise.

Washed my hair in the evening. Contemplated parting it in the middle. Decided not to however because I'm on duty tomorrow and will not have time to alter it if I don't like it.

Shirley's mother moved to Bala in east Wales to get out of London. Bunty recalls spending a few days there: 'There were all these old women in the train carriages talking Welsh, no-one said a word to me.'

Saturday, 6 March

Uncle Chris up for the weekend.

On duty in the morning, altho' as usual I cursed when the alarm went, the morning went pleasantly enough when I got there.

Nancy and I walked for a couple hours in the afternoon – I went home with her for tea and then to the Regal in the evening.

Here we saw a film which before the war we should have despised for its artificiality, but today we enjoy because it is truly escapist.

Dick Powell and Mary Martin singing and enjoying life on some south sea.

'I stand happy go-lucky' it was called.

The film, actually called *Happy Go Lucky*, was a 1943 musical comedy starring Mary Martin as a gold digger who hopes to land a rich husband in Trinidad, but instead gets mixed up with a beach-boy, played by Dick Powell.

Sunday, 7 March

Had two extra in the household today, Uncle Chris and Cousin Dick. Upset Daddy, I'm afraid, by making it clear that we didn't want Uncle Olly to tea as Midge was here.

It probably does seem disgustingly snobbish, but I know just how things get around at Guys, and how catty the girls can be. Even so I do feel rather mean about it and I hope I didn't hurt Daddy's feelings too much.

Tea and supper at Nancy's. The boys from Orchard there and we discussed the forthcoming 'Aid to China' hop which is taking place at Haddon Lodge on the 20th of this month.

Uncle Olly was Bunty's father's brother. Bunty felt he was a tad uncouth and she worried about the impression he might give to her friends. She admits to feeling rather regretful about her attitude.

Orchard House was a boarding house at Dulwich College where students learned oriental languages during the war. Marjory's father was a housemaster there. Haddon Lodge was Nancy's home on Thurlow Park Road in London.

Monday, 8 March

Felt pretty rotten today but think it's because I tried to exist on Vitawheat for breakfast and lunch. I just can't diet but guess I shall never give up trying 'til I lose several stone!

Which in itself would be a miracle.

Felt too tired in the evening to work, so instead had a really early night.

This afternoon we had our anatomy tests back. I got 68% which, considering I knew the answers, was not good enough.

Barnard and Colson and Hodgson-Jones got 80%.

Tuesday, 9 March

I have been feeling quite well again today. Shirley came back after her weekend in Bala, which had been marvellous, she was lucky to have such perfect weather.

Came home one period early because the other half of the class were having practical massage.

Pat phoned to say that Pip was coming home but was meeting her first up in town.

He woke me up at about 2 o'clock and arranged for me to meet him and Pat in Leicester Square Wednesday afternoon. I took in as much as I could, and fell asleep again.

Wednesday, 10 March

Weather still perfect. Pip phoned me at the hospital in the morning and suggested that because of the lovely weather we should walk instead, and he and Pat would meet me in Orpington. This they did, we bus'd to Donnington Manor where we had an excellent lunch.

Then we walked to Shoreham. We were all in fine spirits and the afternoon will remain a very happy memory.

In the evening I had a wonderful surprise. I was presented with a new bike – a Raleigh sports model which I am thrilled with!! What a marvellous family I have!!! Pip left about 8 and I'm afraid we shan't see him again for some time.

Bikes were hard to come by in wartime London, especially a new model. Most of the metal was being used in the weapons industry. Bunty said:

> It was very difficult to get a bike during the war, but my father was good at getting things. When you are in a trade as he was you know lots of other people in other trades, he had very good contacts. Bikes were almost non-existent, I suppose they simply weren't making many of them.

Thursday, 11 March

Came home to lunch because we had a dissection class at Guys in the afternoon. Shirley lunched with me, mother was in town so the company was very welcome.

After the dissection which was helpful but not enjoyable six of us went to the Stoll for a concert. Pam H., Glenys W., Valerie O., Eleanor H and Shirley made up the party and we heard the London Symphony Orchestra playing Tchaikovsky's 5th and the Greig concerto with Moyra Lympany solo piano, it was superb and the seats, altho' balcony, very good. I hope to go again before the season is over.

The dissection Bunty refers to is of human cadavers.

The Stoll was a theatre, formerly the London Opera House and National Theatre, in Westminster. It was closed in 1957 and subsequently demolished to make way for an office block.

Friday, 12 March

Had our long awaited interviews with matron in the morning, Unfortunately, I answered one of her questions with a smile on my face, which she strongly disapproved of. I likewise disapproved of her with her overdone dignity and dictatorial manner – anyway the free afternoon that followed made up for any previous unpleasantness.

I washed my hair then went for a short ride on my new cycle. It was delightful.

In the evening I went to the Regal with Nancy. We saw 'You Were Never Lovelier' which was disappointing.

Had a cup of tea and chat at Haddon Lodge not hurrying home because I'm off duty tomorrow.

You Were Never Lovelier was a 1942 romantic comedy musical starring Fred Astaire and Rita Hayworth. Though it did not meet with Bunty's approval, it was nominated for three Academy Awards.

Saturday, 13 March

This being the last day of the Wings for Victory week I went to Trafalgar Square in the morning to buy some Saving certs. There was a festive air about with an RAF band playing and crowds of people stirred with patriotic feeling at the sight of the big bomber on show there for the occasion.

Mummy and I were at the Williams' for tea and afterwards went to the theatre with Pat and Mrs W.

This was in celebration of Pat's 22nd birthday which is tomorrow. Met Bob and Betty Shaw after the show. They are a very happy couple and, I think, extremely nice.

Wings for Victory week in 1943 was a national week of fundraising for the war effort, themed around the nation's bombers. Members of the public were encouraged to save their money in government accounts through schemes such as war bonds, defence bonds and saving certificates.

Sunday, 14 March

Spent another marvellous day cycling with Peggy and Nancy.

The weather was 100% and nothing marred our enjoyment.

We trained to Sevenoaks and cycled without map or aim, first taking whichever direction looked best. We finished up at Edenbridge, had an enormously amusing journey home, arriving there tired but very pleased with ourselves.

It was the first long ride my new bike has undertaken – it runs perfectly.

Monday, 15 March

Felt pretty tired as a result of yesterday but consider it well worthwhile.

Nothing of interest happened during the day. The weather is still behaving wonderfully. It is being such a marvellous spring that I have doubts about the summer to follow.

Nancy came down in the evening and brought my old bike back which I'd loaned to Peggy yesterday.

Tuesday, 16 March

No entry.

Wednesday, 17 March

Caught the early train home and spent a very lazy afternoon dozing and reading.

Felt guilty about it however because of the phys test tomorrow.

After dinner I settled down to a couple of hours work. Feel I know the phys fairly well.

Thursday, 18 March

Made rather a muck up of the test I'm afraid. Felt rather fed up about it and so phoned Nancy hoping she'd come to the flics to cheer me up.

She was going to Peggy's for the evening so my idea fell thro! But instead I went with her and was very interested in seeing Peggy's room. She has just left her aunt's to live alone in a furnished room. It seemed a very nice place and she very happy about it.

Friday, 19 March

Nothing of interest occurred during the day. Nancy came down for a short time in the evening and took Peggy's new cycle back with her. This cycle is exactly the same as mine and as Daddy was able to get it (ladies bikes being very difficult to get hold of) Peggy is going to have it and pay gradually.

She is very thrilled with it and I am very pleased that we can help her 'cause she is such a grand person.

Saturday, 20 March

On duty in morning. Went round to Nancy's for short time in afternoon to see if I could help with preparations for dance. When I got home found letter from Gordon awaiting me which naturally delighted me.

Pip came home but I didn't see much of him before I left for Haddon Lodge.

Very pleasant dance given in aid of China – boys consisted of students in oriental languages from the college.

It was all very reminiscent of the marvellous pre-war dances we had at Haddon Lodge but Donald's present absence was very prominent.

Sunday, 21 March

Cousin Dick arrived soon after breakfast. We did nothing unusual but spent a very happy afternoon having Pip with us. Pat came to tea and we just sat around the fire talking and listening to Dick's playing until about 8 o'clock when Pip had to leave.

We do not know when next we'll see him 'cause he thinks he is going to Ireland.

Dick left soon after. Nancy came down later and we had a good old discussion about last night's activities.

Monday, 22 March

Back to work with a bit of a Monday morning feeling, possibly increased by heavy wet mist first thing. By lunchtime, however, sun was shining and we ate our lunch in the garden at Everdon.

Felt a bit tired during the afternoon and my mood was not improved by having two anatomy lectures, one on top of other – then a free period when Camey gave us a question on R.A. to do.

It is impossible to work on these occasions the time was wasted and question will have to be done at home.

Camey was Ms Cameron, a lecturer, who questioned her class about rheumatoid arthritis (RA).

Tuesday, 23 March

Again the day started badly with heavy mist but was lovely by lunchtime. Collins and Keane were discharged so I finished fairly early. The afternoon passed pleasantly enough and as I was amongst the half of the class not doing practical treatment with Camey I came home one period early.

Found a marvellous photo of Donald Campbell waiting for me on arrival home. I was so thrilled with it that I have already written to thank him.

Wednesday, 24 March

Today I played truant from the hospital and spent a grand day at Brighton with Mummy, Daddy and Uncle Chris. The ban prohibiting visitors to Brighton begins at the end of this month so we thought we'd get in while the going's good.

It was lovely to smell the sea again after two years even tho' the defences prevented us seeing much of it.

We had a nice enough lunch at the Ship Hotel and spent the afternoon walking almost the entire length of the promenade, then back to the Ship for tea and home about 8.30. It's been a wonderful day.

Brighton, a town on England's south coast, was heavily fortified as a defence zone during the war due to the threat of a German sea invasion.

The beaches were mined and fenced off with barbed wire. Sections of piers were removed to stop them from being used as landing points for invaders.

Important pieces of art and collections from the town's museum were moved into the countryside.

To limit the number of people in the town and therefore the number of potential casualties in the event of an invasion, several bans were introduced during the Second World War. During the banning periods, only people with relatives in Brighton were allowed to visit the town.

Brighton was hit by German bombers fifty-six times between 1940 and 1944, in which nearly 200 people were killed.

Thursday, 25 March

Woke up to find a miserably wet morning. Had cleared up by lunchtime and owing presumably to my early night last night I felt in very good spirits. If only I had the will to go to bed early every night I'm sure I'd be a much more pleasant person.

Nancy and Pat popped in during the evening. Nancy had a letter from Donald with her which referred to my 'typical bored expression' which is quite untrue and I strongly resent.

That so called bored expression is usually covering uneasiness on my part! But still, I must make the effort to correct it.

Friday, 26 March

Posted letter to Donald (airmail).

Started new scheme of large scale exercise classes in the wards. It is Mr Bachelor's idea and seems quite successful.

Read our physiology tests back in the afternoon and my worst fears were fulfilled by only getting 19/40.

In the evening I went to The Regal with Mummy and Midge where we saw an excellent programme.

Desert Victory, a film which made me burst with pride for the 8th army. I don't remember any film before causing in me so much tension, It deals with the success in Egypt at the end of 1942 ending with the taking of Tripoli. With it was Ralph Richardson in The Silverfleet.

Desert Victory was a documentary produced by the British Ministry of Information. It covered the Allies' battles in North Africa against Rommel and the Afrika Korps. It relied heavily on captured German newsreel footage.

The Silver Fleet was a 1943 film starring Ralph Richardson as a Dutch shipyard owner who struggles with the morals of collaborating with the Nazis.

Saturday, 27 March

This morning I had my hair permed at Pratts. It was as usual a long and tedious process but the result well worth it. It really looks very nice and is so much less trouble.

I only hope it doesn't grow out too soon.

Nancy phoned today that Willie J. Hester alias Texas Dan had arrived at Haddon Lodge and that I was to go up immediately and make his acquaintance.

I've heard so much about him since Nancy and Peggy met him in the Cotswolds that it was fun seeing him. Diana also turned up and we went to the flics in the evening, Natasha, a Russian film we saw, was really excellent!

Texas Dan was an American soldier or GI, of whom Bunty said, 'They were quite flirtatious.'

About three million US troops passed through Britain during the war, bringing with them the luxuries of America such as sweets and stockings. They also earned about five times as much as their British counterparts, and were said to be very generous. Almost 70,000 British women married US GIs.

Sunday, 28 March

Went to tea with Nancy. The three Scotch boys – Harry, Donald and Billy – were there. Their time at the college ends next Thursday and from there they go into the services, so it's the last time we'll see them for a while.

We had a very happy day playing around the garden (if only it had been Michael, Donald and Kenneth) as we used to and listening to the gramophone – chatting, giggling and enjoying ourselves generally. I don't mean that I dislike the Scotch boys when I say I wish they were D. M. and K. I just mean it would denote pre-war times.

Monday, 29 March

Renewed train season ticket for one month i.e. until April 27th.

Three items of good news today:

1. *the 8th army have taken the Mareth Line. Montgomery holds everybody's greatest admiration!*

2.   *Daddy has managed to book a room at a hotel in Guildford for Mummy and I to spend a few days during my easter holiday. Knowing how crowded the place is we rather doubted any success.*

3.   *Margery phoned this evening asking me if I'd like to go to a dance at Ivyholme tomorrow night. I'm not sure if this is altogether good news because I don't like going out during the week – especially this week as I've a theory test on Thursday – but still, dances are so rare nowadays and I might enjoy it! This factor always hangs in the balance.*

Ivyholme was a boarding house at Dulwich College.

Tuesday, 30 March

Well the dance has been fun – great fun! Why does it always happen that when an arrangement is 'last moment' and not much looked forward to it's invariably a success. Met two pleasant boys – Monty somebody and Gordon Carry. What's more, they seemed to like me!!

I danced quite a lot, and talked a good deal, and was in a much more confident mood when I left than when I arrived! Gordon C. walked home with me. He lives in Edinburgh and is one of the Ivyholme students that is studying Chinese or Japanese – I can't remember which. He is going home in a few days time for a month's holiday.

Wednesday, 31 March

Repaired stockings and lazed in the afternoon deciding to do my theory revision in the evening.

Margery phoned – would I go round to the Orchard for a farewell party the boys were going at 9.ocl. Naturally all thoughts of theory test went to the wind!

When I arrived I renewed my acquaintance with Monty, we got on very well together and the result was another highly successful evening!!

Sardines and murder were the main games – so like those old parties we gave when at school.

The proportions were rather in our favour that is about five girls and twenty five boys! Monty took me home and my opinion of him went up the longer I was with him. It's a pity he has finished his course at Dulwich.

Thursday, 1 April

Felt very elated after my unexpected social activities and to my surprise didn't feel unduly tired. The theory test was rather confusing but then theory is.

Nancy came down in the evening and we had a grand old expounding of news and doings. She had been out with Cyril from Ivyholme last night and had so missed the Orchard farewell party, nevertheless I think she enjoyed herself as much as I did.

I am feeling increasingly sorry that I didn't meet Monty earlier on during his period in Dulwich. Just my luck that it should be the last two days of his course!! Wrote to him re my cigarette lighter!!!!

Bunty said: 'I probably told a little white lie, something like "did I leave my cigarette lighter with you?". I think I was probably being a bit devious, making up an excuse to see him again.'

Friday, 2 April

The day itself passed uneventfully. I am beginning to feel the reaction of my late nights but shall continue to say they were worth it.

In the evening Nancy and I met Peggy and we passed a very pleasant couple of hours at the Shanghai. Chinese food is most interesting and we all ate colossal meals capped by chrysanthemum tea!

The atmosphere made me very tired so I came straight home, chatted with the folks for a bit – and so to bed.

Saturday, 3 April

Had breakfast in bed. Sent off Gordon's Epoulettes and the order for his polyfotos – very belated effort I'm afraid. Being a wonderful spring day I went for a walk with Nancy in the afternoon.

In the evening we two, plus Barbara M. went to Victoria and saw Casablanca, an extremely worthwhile film. Got home to find Cousin Dick in residence. Tonight we put the clocks on an hour.

Gordon Russell was a member of the Royal New Zealand Navy who stayed with the Leatherdales.

Barbara M was Barbara Morton.

Sunday, 4 April

1st D.M.

Wrote to Tony in the morning. We've had many unexpected visitors today. Namely Cousins Doris and Olive and their respective husbands, and Brian Stott who is on embarkation leave. I went for a short walk this afternoon as the weather was so perfect.

In the evening I attended a hen party at Margery's. This was quite pleasant but I cannot say I like Jean's friends. Pat W. was at home when I returned. Betty had sent me up some film rolls!!!

Monday, 5 April

Posted airmail letter to Tony.

The weather today has been almost like midsummer, I sunbathed on the lawn at Everdon during lunch period and we also had our exercise class out there. Feeling rather tired I had decided to go to bed at 9.30. However an excellent play on the wireless has ruined my good intentions and it is now 11 o'clock and I am just in bed.

The play was by Val Gielgud and Constance Cummings, Hugh Sinclair and Maurice Goring were in it – could I possibly have missed it?!

Tuesday, 6 April

Started the day well by receiving an answer from Monty. It was a very satisfactory letter – the morning went quite pleasantly altho' I seem to have developed a bit of a heady cold.

The afternoon dragged deplorably – I certainly need a holiday – oh boy! For Easter!!

Wrote to Monty in the evening telling him that I had found my lighter!

Wednesday, 7 April

Read that a Keith Wade has been killed in Canada. It must be our friend of tennis club days.

Met Daddy and Gladys Kennet at Troc for lunch. Sat near Naughton Wayne and his wife in the afternoon, we saw the Merry Widow but I fear this type of show doesn't appeal to me enormously. In spite of this I enjoyed the outing immensely.

Gordon's original polyfoto order arrived after all these months so we have now several surplus photos of him. I must remember to send one to his mother and one to Margaret as I've promised. Nancy called in in the evening. I wrote to Gordon.

The Kennets were the Leatherdales' next-door neighbours. Naughton Wayne was a well-known actor.

Thursday, 8 April

Have a heady sort of cold hanging over me and after a rather disturbed night felt wretched most of the day. At lunchtime I posted Gordon's letter – had to send it ordinary mail unfortunately because there's no airmail service to his present address. It is – M.L. 471 C/o G.P.D. – London.

Shall go to bed now, 10 o'clock, and get a reasonably early night.

Friday, 9 April

Came home early because it didn't mean missing much and my cold was making me feel pretty grim – collected my new world symphony records before leaving Orpington.

Have heard two pieces of news today. Firstly Gladys Kennet is engaged to Denis somebody, a friend of Regis in the FAA. Secondly the Williams have heard bad news of Geoff. This is all we know at present and are most desperately anxious to know more. It doesn't seem possible that anything too awful can have happened to him – the suggestion of it has shocked me very much.

Geoff Williams was in the army. The bad news was that he was reported missing in action.

Saturday, 10 April

On duty in the morning. Nancy phoned at lunchtime to say she again had Texas Dan in residence and would I go to tea? I did, and so did Margery. In the evening the four of us went to the Metropol at Victoria and saw 'Star Spangled Rhythm' – great fun.

I thought it very gallant of Texas to take three girls out but he seemed to quite enjoy the situation!

Went back to Nancy's for supper and finally got home at 12.30 – Pip came home earlier in the evening.

Sunday, 11 April

We had quite a household in the afternoon. Pip, Dick Gulley, who is on ten days leave, Margery, the Norwood Partridges and Pat. Incidentally, Geoff listed as wounded which may not be much, thank goodness. We had a very pleasant day. Nancy called in the evening for a short time. She and Peggy had been cycling. I had intended going with them until I heard Pip was coming home – they appeared to have had a good time – Pip left very late.

Monday, 12 April

Rather a Monday morning feeling crowned by a busy morning. We are all looking forward desperately for our coming holiday.

Worked a bit at anatomy in the evening and intend to get to bed comparatively early.

It is now 10.15 and as Midge is waiting to come in here i.e. the bathroom, I'll get to bed.

Tuesday, 13 April

Today the weather has been wonderful! We sunbathed at Everdon at lunchtime and the sun was terrifically hot. I did not stay for practical massage, will stay on Friday instead.

Got home to find that Mummy was intending to clear out the pantry for the painters. It hasn't been done since we came here, about fourteen years ago, and gosh! What a job. It took Daddy, Mummy and myself two hours good work. I felt very weary and dirty afterwards – so I bathed and went to bed early.

Wednesday, 14 April

We received a charming photo of cousin Pauline today.

Had an unusual job this morning. Mr Smith had his plaster off and Miss Stevens ordered a bath for his leg and olive oil massage. She said 'sit him on the edge of the bath!' This I was dubious about as I had visions of him falling in, or out, so I erected a sort of seat inside the bath. It was all very amusing and little 'Smith' was most impressed.

Very warm afternoon so I sat in the garden and did some anatomy revision. The evening was beautiful so I went for a walk with Nancy. The blossom is indescribably beautiful this year.

Thursday, 15 April

Another boiling hot day. Sunbathed during lunch period and it was superb.

Had our anatomy test in the afternoon which I'm afraid I mucked by failing to answer the 'invertors of foot' question fully.

The door was opened to me by Pip who had popped up on a short pass. He goes to Ireland tomorrow. Pat came up and Nancy later. Dick Gulley also present. We had a happy evening all together and I bid farewell to Pip about 11.30 as bed was urgently calling.

Friday, 16 April

Washed my hair first time since perm tonight. This weather is unbelievable. Today it has been absolutely midsummer! We had both lectures this afternoon in the garden taking notes lying on the grass under the trees! It was perfect!

The first week's holiday starts tomorrow so today's lectures are the last for two weeks.

Went for a walk with Nancy in the evening. Met Daphne Salter and Lyle Downing who were 'billing and cooing' rather obviously. Called in and spent half an hour at Margery's.

'Billing and cooing' was another way of saying flirting.

Saturday, 17 April

During the night we had a slight air-raid.

Heat wave still at its height. I was not on duty this morning so got up fairly early and made for Lewis' – Gower St. Here I ordered and I paid for a Tidy medical book. Then to the West End where I bought birthday presents for auntie Queenie, Barbara Morton and an easter present for Mummy. Then to St James Theatre to book seats for 'A month in the country'.

In the evening I went to the Rialto with Nancy and Margery. Saw a pretty good film – 'Tomorrow We Live', John Clements and Hugh Sinclair.

Auntie Queenie was Nancy's mother. *Tomorrow We Live* was a 1943 film about the French Resistance's efforts against the Nazis.

Sunday, 18 April

There was a short alert at 10.30 in evening.

Another indescribably happy day spent cycling in Surrey with Nancy and Peggy. The weather has been terrific – cloudless blue skies, the superb spring flowers and blossom, everything looking its best.

We started at Dorking and, unsurprisingly, ended there and got home early without any 'incidents'. I cannot remember a more lovely spring than this one we are having now. How I wish Gordon and Dudley were here to see what an English spring can be here.

The air-raid alert at 10.30 pm did not develop into anything. The 'incident' Bunty, Nancy and Peggy avoided was not running into any boys.

Monday, 19 April

Had a marvellous 'surprise' evening – Vernon Small old school pal of Dudley Bird's I met about a year ago, phoned and arranged to meet me. I remembered so little about him that I was rather dubious about the outcome of the arrangement, but my doubts were all ill founded. With two friends of his – an American pilot and his girlfriend Phyllis – the four of us dined at Shephards Tavern off Piccadilly then went on a refined 'pub crawl'! I had my first view of inside The Ritz, and various other establishments couldn't believe it was me out with two such good looking officers!!

The Ritz in Piccadilly is arguably one of London's most famous hotels, a swanky affair, which, since its opening in 1906, has been a favourite of the wealthy members of high society.

Tuesday, 20 April

Have been in excellent humour today as a result of last night. Got home from Orpington about 4.30 – had dinner with Midge, then we set out to see 'A Month in the Country' with Michael Redgrave – it was the sort of day I enjoy enormously, M.R.'s performance being as superb as ever.

We passed the scene of some of last night's activities en route to the theatre in the form of the Rye and Dry Club, Bury Street. The likelihood of seeing Vernon was very remote but I must confess I had hoped.

Wednesday, 21 April

Had intended to go into town this afternoon but a delayed action hangover changed my mind for me.

Instead I went straight home from the hospital, had a sleep and spent a lazy afternoon. Went for a walk with Nancy in the evening – in spite of rather unpleasant rainy weather.

Received letter from Dudley and Gordon in some post. Former contained photos, latter a cutting about Pauline's engagement and 21st which mother deduces hasn't occurred yet.

Pauline was a relative who lived in New Zealand.

Thursday, 22 April

Finished work this morning for ten days – yippee!! Went up to town this afternoon and bought R.A.F. wings to hang on my charm bracelet. It's from Mummy for easter. Also bought four records of Bing, Bob Hope and Celia Lipton.

We had a letter from Pip, his first since reaching Ireland. First impressions seem to be quite good.

I wrote to him in the evening. Also wrote to thank V.S. for Monday, doubt whether address will find him.

Received a letter from Pip to Pat in the evening. Nancy at home when I got back.

Friday, 23 April (Good Friday)

Drove, with Daddy, to Kennington Lane Shop in the morning. It was heavenly to be in the car again! I collected some 'hot-cross buns' and took some to Nancy at

Lombard St and some to the staff at City Rd. Here things had changed slightly, Mr Vincent having left and a new cashier in his place.

In the afternoon I distributed some more buns because there are not many about this year. Took some to the Gayfords, the Campbells and Gladys.

Pat, Dick and Nancy with us in the evening. Dick tells us he's asked Nellie to marry him.

The Leatherdales' main bakery was at Kennington Lane. At its peak the company, which was started in 1870 by Bunty's grandfather, owned twelve shops in central London and supplied bread to Harrods. The company closed in the 1950s.

The Gayfords were Margery's family. Dick was close friends with Nellie and her husband who had sadly died. Dick then proposed to her.

Saturday, 24 April

Mother and I went to Streatham in the morning and at Pratt's obtained a pretty pale blue crepe frock. It seems to suit me rather well, colour and shape – also bought a glamorous pair of cami knickers.

Met Nancy and Peggy after lunch and we saw 'The Gentle Sex!' a film about the a.t.s.

Margery joined us afterwards and we had supper at the 'Shanghai'. As usual it was great fun – we had intended to go home after this, but when passing a film with Tommy Trinder in – 'The Bells Go Down', decided to make a night of it.

Pratt's was a department store in Streatham.

The Gentle Sex was a 1943 film directed by Leslie Howard about seven British schoolgirls who decide to do their bit for the war, so they join the Auxiliary Territorial Services (ATS).

The Bells Go Down was a production of the famous Ealing Studios. The 1943 film featured the comedian Tommy Trinder in a serious role as an auxiliary fireman battling blazes during the Blitz.

Sunday, 25 April (Easter Day)

Daddy woke me with a cup of tea and two pretty gold charms for my bracelet, an elephant from him and a yacht from Mummy – my bracelet becomes more interesting with each addition.

Nancy came to tea and we spent one of the quietest Easter Days I remember, just the four of us. It is the first Easter that Pip has not spent with us I think – Nancy and I went for walks before and after tea and spent the rest of the time listening to the gramophone.

Monday, 26 April (Easter Monday)

The Partridges from Norwood came for the afternoon and evening. Janet brought a friend Wendy with her – an extremely pleasant girl.

In the evening Janet, Wendy, Nancy, Margery and myself went to Brixton Astoria. We saw quite an amusing film – 'I Married a Witch' – but the day wasn't a patch on our usual Bank Holiday. What a difference it makes not having the car on these occasions.

The usual bank holiday activity was to go out on a family trip in the car, which was usually reserved for business only matters.

I Married a Witch was an American comedy film made in 1942, starring Veronica Lake as a 17th century witch who has come back to life and tries to make Fredric March's Wallace Woolley fall in love with her as punishments for his ancestor's persecution of her.

Tuesday, 27 April

Had my hair set at Pratt's in the morning then met Mummy at Waterloo.

We arrived at the Lion Hotel Guildford at lunchtime to find it very crowded and muddled and we were not pleased to have to wait 1/2 hour for lunch.

In the afternoon we tramped the town and decided it was a lovely old town – after dinner we went to a flic. This being the only thing to do, this holiday will be a rest if nothing else.

Wednesday, 28 April

Walked to Shalford in the morning – met a couple of rather nice girls also staying at the Lion en route.

In the afternoon I went for a walk by myself along a towpath by the River Wye. Unfortunately it was early closing in Guildford and rather like Brighton on Bank Holiday! Pam Herbertson and Hester Wilkes turned up in the evening having been cycling all day. We had a very pleasant evening together at the hotel.

Thursday, 29 April

In the morning I took mother on the towpath walk I'd discovered yesterday. Much nicer today because it was deserted.

In the afternoon we took a bus to Ewhurst. Dear old Ewhurst, visited on two previous cycle rides. Had tea at our little guest house and took a different bus route back thro' Shere.

Went for a walk in the evening although it was raining and rather dismal.

Friday, 30 April

Yesterday, while we were waiting for the bus a conductress confronted us with a 'do you remember me Mrs Leatherdale!' Mummy did – it was our old nurse. I didn't remember her but she was very charming and I liked her immensely.

Today it has rained all day, in the evening we watched a dance at the hotel. Also watching was a girl called Joy Watson who was an old Streatham Hill High School girl. Before my time actually but quite a coincidence.

Saturday, 1 May

Had a lovely day today, going to the Hogs Back Hotel for lunch. Decided that this is definitely the place for us another time.

Pre-war courtesy and service and such a modern, well designed place.

Walked halfway back to Guildford, then caught 6.20 fast train back to Waterloo. Daddy greeted us with lovely meal of eggs and bacon – haven't had it since we've been away.

Bunty and Nancy used to go to the Hogs Back Hotel to ride horses.

Sunday, 2 May

Feel rather depressed about work again tomorrow. Feel that I've just got to study harder in the future or I'll never have a chance with the exam. I do hope I've not bitten off more than I can chew.

Walked in the afternoon with Nancy. Dick here for dinner and tea, he has one stripe now – but seems worried about Nellie's answer, I hadn't believed he was so fond of her.

Monday, 3 May

Back to work after holiday. Had a Monday morning feeling with capital M, but it cleared off fairly quickly. Learned that myself and seven others of the set have been selected to sell hospital day flags tomorrow. Don't know how the selection was made but I'm very pleased that I'm one of the eight. It should be great fun especially as its to be in the Regent Street district. Everything at hospital much the same.

Tuesday, 4 May

Midge starts her exams today.

At hospital 'til 10.30 when I left (with others of flag-selling party) to catch Charing X train. Went to depot which was at Liberty's where we found little old Mrs Johnson in residence. She gave us luncheon tickets value 1/3d which we disposed of at Lyon's. Sold flags in Soho area until about 2.40 when I chanced to meet Mummy. She Glenys W. and myself had tea at Quality Inn, then Mummy went home and Glenys and I went shop gazing. I bought zodiac charm for my bracelet and two pairs of stockings.

Wednesday, 5 May

Had a full morning and had to catch late train home. Mrs Nicholson gave me my lunch as Mummy and Daddy were out.

Made up yesterday's missed lectures in the afternoon until Midge came home from her exam – after dinner, the evening being so peaceful and still, I went for a long walk. Pat was calling when I arrived home so she stayed and we chatted the rest of the evening away. Midge and I went to bed and soon after M&D arrived home.

Thursday, 6 May

A rather tiring day today. In the middle of the afternoon we had over an hour and a half without lectures, Steve being away and Wareham late getting back from Guys. It was very annoying because with everyone chatting work is impossible and its just a waste of time.

Actually I had H.V. Morton 'Atlantic Meeting' with me which certainly made the period less of a bore.

I got to bed fairly early because the 'curse' was having its effect.

Steve was Ms Stephens, another lecturer. The curse was Bunty's phrase for her period.

Friday, 7 May

Mother went to bed early with a rather nasty pain.

Said 'goodbye' to little Mr Smith this morning who is going home on Saturday.

Only had two periods this afternoon so was able to get home, change and have a snack before setting out for the theatre with Nancy. Had lunch at the B.R. with Moira, Pam and Hester and it had been a very riotous meal, each one of us feeling definitely 'weekendy'!

The play this evening has been marvellous! John Gielgud and a splendid cast in a comedy 'Love for love' by Congrieve. It was terrific!!!

Saturday, 8 May

Marvellous victory in Egypt! Tunis captured!

In spite of very undecided weather Nancy and I carried out our arrangement to ride at Dorking. Wind and rain didn't spoil a superb 1 1/2 hours on Bruce. My previous dislike of him was practically cured.

Ate sandwiches on Box Hill for lunch and walked in the afternoon. We had tea at the 'Railway Arms' and then caught a train home.

Mother has been in bed today with a pain that sounds like rheumatism. I worked in the evening, a couple of hours good hard work in physiology.

Sunday, 9 May

A wet, windy, morning cancelled our arrangements to go cycling. Instead I joined in the house running, mother being in bed. Daddy cooked the meals and Midge and I cleared up his mess!!

In the afternoon the weather cleared and Peggy, Nancy and myself took a train to Epsom. I was in a rather low mood which wouldn't clear off. We walked for about 10 miles, were unable to get tea and arrived home very tired in the evening, am afraid I was irritable and unsociable while out.

Monday, 10 May

No entry.

Tuesday, 11 May

No entry.

Wednesday, 12 May

Today I had lunch at the Wayside and caught a train whereby I got to the Haymarket Theatre about 2.15. Here I met Mummy, Daddy and Pat W. This is the last time we shall be out with Pat while she is still a civilian.

We saw a superb new Noel Coward play – 'This Happy Breed' – it is the family history of a lower middle class suburban family between the two wars. It is the first I've seen N.C. act on the stage and I was most impressed Then to a rather poor flic and on to dinner at the Troc. It was a very happy day.

Pat had joined the Auxiliary Territorial Service, which was the woman's branch of the army.

Thursday, 13 May

The physiology test we were supposed to have today was postponed earlier in the week to next Thursday. So the day passed normally enough.

In the evening I cycled down to Pat's with a watch we were giving her as a 'joining up' present. She seemed very pleased with it. When I arrived she was sorting out what she was taking with her and seemed rather dejected, I expect she'll soon be enjoying it however when she gets over first strangeness.

Friday, 14 May

Pat caught the 7.30 train this morning to N. Wales where she had to report on this her first day of service life – Good luck, Paddles, if, in this new life, you find someone you like better than Pip, be very gentle with him because he loves you very much and I'm afraid losing you would have a very shattering effect on him.

Learned this afternoon that I'm having first summer holiday ie from July 5th   Aug 3rd. All the rest of the gang, except Shirley, are the same.

Saturday, 15 May

On duty in the morning – a boiling day and I wore as little as was decent.

After lunch I sunbathed until Nancy turned up. Mother's sciatica was very painful again, Dr Kinmouth seems to be disinterested, more keen on getting mother back on injections for her heart.

Not that there is much wrong with it, but I'm afraid he is becoming commercially minded.

Went with Nancy and Peggy to the Regal Streatham where we saw a rather feeble programme – 'Keeper of the flame'.

The sciatica Bunty's mother was suffering from turned out to be an early sign of the cancer which killed her in 1951 at the age of 63.

Sunday, 16 May

Mother in bed this morning, her so-called sciatica having come again. Because of this I cancelled arrangement to ride at Dorking. I stayed at home doing a bit of house work for a change.

Nellie came to tea in the afternoon. She and Dick don't behave as one expects newly engaged couples to behave, possibly because they're well over the age of discretion!

Had supper at Nancy's and met an ATS from the AA battery on the golf course whom they had invited to Haddon Lodge. She is very charming.

The AA is the anti-aircraft defences.

Monday, 17 May

Last night was disturbed by three air raid alerts. The second was quite noisy and we were undecided about going downstairs. I find I am much more scared of air raids now since I've seen the results of so many at Orpington than I was during the blitz. My imagination seems to have been sharpened. The weather has been lovely again today and we had anatomy and exercises in the garden.

About ten people were killed during the three raids carried out by twenty German aircraft on Greater London and Essex. The *London Evening Standard* said a Mr Gray, 62, died in the first raid, killed shortly after going to bed.

'Rescuers said his newly-made widow, who had watched her husband go upstairs shortly before a single fighter hit their home reducing it to ruins, showed great courage and was cracking jokes with them', the paper reported.

Others killed included Harry Taylor, 69, his wife Blanche Taylor, 68, and two unidentified people.

Three died in an Anderson shelter which was blown over. Mr and Mrs Reed, Miss L. Stone, and Mr and Mrs Roman were killed in another part of London. One child was found dead in a hit house. A canary in a battered birdcage in the same home had survived though.

One other story of note comes from East Anglia, where a Mr Cecil Bocking returned to his bomb-damaged home to see what he could salvage. He heard a voice say 'hallo boy' from beneath some debris. About four-feet down he found his 25-year-old parrot. After being fed and watered, the revived bird apparently began 'talking away as if nothing had happened'.

Tuesday, 18 May

More air raids during night, nothing very bad but presumably they are to show the Nazis' rage at the RAF bombing of the great dams in the Ruhr on Saturday night. A very large area has been flooded at great interference to the industrial work going on there. It indubitably is a great success, but the thought of all those civilians drowned is not the type of victory I like best.

Twelve people were killed when a bomb fell in a road, reported the *London Evening Standard*.

'A baby was found alive and well in her cot just yards away from her dead mother, Mrs Wilkinson, after a high explosive bomb smashed two houses in a London suburb,' the paper said.

Also killed that night were Iris Wright, aged 11, who was at a friend's house, and five members of the Rees family. Three of the enemy planes were brought down.

The RAF's raids on three dams in the Ruhr became an iconic success story for the Allies.

Lancaster bombers destroyed dams at the Mohne, Eder and Sorte reservoirs, which contained about two-thirds of all the water in the Ruhr area of western Germany.

Wednesday, 19 May

More air raids last night, but apart from breaking one's rest they do little damage.

Caught an early train home and was glad to get there because the weather is still very hot. Managed to get quite brown in the garden in the afternoon. In the evening we heard Churchill's speech from USA.

It was splendid and the Americans gave him such a terrific reception that I felt very proud of being English. This may sound sentimental but it really did stir me enormously.

Thursday, 20 May

Phys test cancelled again. Instead we had two afternoon lectures then went up to Guys to hear a lecture on artificial limbs from a Mr Carter (I think it was) of Roehampton. I had time to get home and tell mother, who was back in bed with her sciatica being rather troublesome.

The lecture was fairly interesting and I'm glad I didn't miss it, altho' the premiere of an Eric Portman film was a great temptation and nearly made me do so – there were a few light raids again last night.

Friday, 21 May

A raidless night – the first this week.

I have caught an irritating cold, it may even be hayfever, anyway it blocks my head and makes me feel rather muzzy.

This afternoon we had a tremendously amusing exercise class with Camey, for tonsils and adenoids – she took the class using us as children between three and five. It was great fun and really very instructive.

I went to bed at eight o'clock feeling headachy.

The *London Evening Standard* on Friday, May 21 reported the last five nights had been disturbed by air raids but 'no enemy aircraft appeared. Raiders were turned back after being seen off the coast,' the paper said.

Saturday, 22 May

On duty this morning. Dr Kinmouth saw mother today and ordered her to stay in bed until Monday. She's feeling much better and doesn't like the idea but it will definitely do her good.

Went to Streatham after lunch and bought a fuchsia box jacket for knocking around in. It's really quite nice.

Supper with Nancy, then to see 'The Ghostbreakers' with her. I've seen it before but starring Bob Hope could go on seeing it indefinitely.

Sunday, 23 May

A Sunday of household duties. Mr, Mrs and Joan Goulding came round in the morning. Sally, Joan's little daughter, is in hospital after falling in a bath of boiling soda water – the poor little thing is badly burnt, but luckily not on her face.

Diana and Nancy came to tea in the afternoon, Diana and I chatting enthusiastically about our coming holiday – if we ever get away – booking up is proving so very difficult and I fear we've left it rather late.

Monday, 24 May

No entry.

Tuesday, 25 May

Today we drew for five of us to go to Farnborough soon. All the gang except myself were lucky and I am despairing at the thought of being at Orpington without any of my pals.

Shall ask Wareham if she can arrange for me to go too.

Rushed to catch the train to town where I was meeting Daddy and Midge at the theatre. Shirley used a ticket we had originally got for Mummy, who is still in bed.

Saw John Clements in 'July came to a city' by Priestly. I thought it disappointing. We had dinner after at Casa Pepes. The whole evening was a farewell to Midge.

Farnborough was another hospital in North East Hampshire where the trainee physiotherapists would be sent to do gynaecology work.

Wednesday, 26 May

Caught the early train home to find that Mrs Nicholson had not been in and with Mummy still in bed this was no joke. Midge had managed the house in the morning but she left early in the afternoon for Clacton where she is spending a few days before coming back to Orpington for her electrical.

It has been very nice having her here. She is a great sport and rarely irritating. There are few people I should have liked better living with us. Lazed the rest of the day and walked with Nancy in the evening.

Mrs Nicholson was the Leatherdales' housekeeper. Midge was an older physio who had lived with the Leatherdales, her electrical was one of her final exams. Bunty recalls:

We always had people living with us, they had nowhere else to go and we had a very big house. Eight bedrooms, three big double rooms with a dressing room, then four on the top floor. One was Mary's, our live-in cook, one was my playroom and one was Peter's. There was another bedroom which I used to go to in the summer, it was from there I saw Crystal Palace burn down in 1936.

Thursday, 27 May

Am still unable to find out if I can go to Farnborough because Wareham did not come to Everdon today. The suspense is killing me! The rest of the gang are very sweet about it and appear to be as anxious as I am.

Had the often put-off phys test in the afternoon. It wasn't very difficult but that by no means suggests that I did well. Felt very depressed in the evening thinking how frightful it will be at Orpington without the others.

Friday, 28 May

To my intense relief I have been allowed to go to Farnboro' next Wednesday. Wareham was charming about it, Camey also. Why did I ever doubt them!

Now I've got to start worrying about the newness of Farnboro' and whether it'll be very difficult!

In the evening I walked to Streatham and saw 'The Tales of Manhattan' a really very good film.

On the way home I called in at Haddon Lodge. Not being on duty tomorrow enabled me to forget about bed time for once.

The Tales of Manhattan was a 1942 romance and comedy about a cursed tailcoat and the lives of those who wore it.

Saturday, 29 May

Received letter from Gordon.

Breakfast in bed in the morning – brought up to me by Daddy!! Caught the 1.34 train to Sevenoaks where I spent an extremely enjoyable time playing tennis with Moira Pam and Hester!

I met Mrs Simpson who is a most charming lady looking like an older edition of Betty Williams. I fell completely for their cottage which is truly old but very fresh and clean and tastefully furnished.

Pam and I on the journey home, fully discussed nearly everyone of the gang! Very enlightening!!

Mrs Simpson was Moira's mother, Moira being a friend of Bunty's.

Sunday, 30 May

Dick in residence. In the afternoon he met Nellie who came to tea. She asked me to be bridesmaid at her wedding which should be quite fun!! Simply can't think seriously of Dick being married. He seems such a confirmed bachelor!

Saw Harry Dudgeon in the evening, he is spending a short weekend pass at Nancy's being now in the army and stationed at Warley-Essex. Monty Ainslie is also there and I can't help thinking how useful it would have been if things were still normal with my relations there!

Monday, May 31

No entry.

Tuesday, 1 June

The new JUNIOR set arrived at Orpington today – they are a large set about 26. I showed some of them patients of mine that they are taking over – said goodbye to my patients, Maynard and Mr Gardner appeared sincerely sorry I was going, as indeed I am re themselves.

Got home early in the afternoon and scanned the adverts in the Sunday Times for new holiday addresses to try. I wrote to four places, desperately hoping to get in somewhere.

Wednesday, 2 June

First day at Farnboro' and one of the most tiring, nerve-racking mornings I have ever spent in my life! The only pleasant thought I have to go on is that everybody seems to hate it at first and like it later on.

Went up to Piccadilly at lunchtime and scanned the shops for a silver wedding present for Auntie Q. and Uncle Donald. Finally bought a small silver tray at Perry's, Regent St.

Thursday, 3 June

Another nerve-racking morning at Farnboro! Lunched at the Candy Cafe (an establishment I think I'll patronise a good deal) then to Grays for dissections which I found as distasteful as ever.

In the evening Mummy, Daddy and I went to the Campbells to celebrate their 25 years of married life. Diana up there and we had further discussions re holiday. She seemed to like the idea of Exmouth.

Bunty does not have fond memories of dissections at Gray's:

There was restaurant next door and you could smell fish and chips, it put me off fish and chips. Other girls would be hacking away but I used to stand back and not get involved. I was a bit squeamish but it was a good way to learn where things were in the body.

Friday, 4 June

Farnboro' getting slightly less terrifying, but still bad enough. Before I left home in the morning, two nice things happened! 1) a letter from Tony, He may be coming home soon! 2) Pip arrived home looking very fit for 12 days leave.

Also I had a reply from Devoncourt Hotel, Exmouth, saying they could accommodate us. I accepted this. Pip and I spent a couple of hours at Haddon Lodge in the evening. Texas there for a short while.

Saturday, 5 June

Went with Pip to Brentwood for the day. We called on all our relations there and were treated very well. It was particularly nice to see Jill and Teddy again.

As Pip was meeting Pat at Paddington (her first 48 hrs leave since joining the A.T.S.) I took myself to the flics at Leicester Square. Very much enjoyed 'We dive at dawn' with Eric Portman. Had a meal at 'Quality Inn' afterwards. Things were a little strained at home when I got there. Don't know why.

Jill and Teddy were more cousins on Bunty's mother's side. Jill subsequently married an English engineer called Roger and the pair moved to Canada.

We Dive At Dawn was a 1943 film about a British submarine crew who chase a new German warship so far that they don't have enough fuel to get home.

Sunday, 6 June

Saw Pat in the morning for first time since her call-up. As I expected she looked immaculate and chic in her uniform – we saw little of Pip for the rest of the day.

The Upper Norwood Partridges, Dick and Nellie came to tea. In the evening I went for a fairly long walk with Janet. I was disappointed that I hadn't gone cycling with Peggy and Nancy. I put this off because Pip was on leave – but of course I hadn't bargained for him being at the Williams all day – altho' t'was only natural as Pat was only on 48 hrs.

Monday, 7 June

Had my first moderately enjoyable morning at Farnboro'. At least I wasn't completely miserable as last week.

At lunchtime I registered, should have done this on Saturday but didn't have time then. Felt a bit under weather in the afternoon and was glad to get home.

Wrote to Mrs Knowles in the evening to see if she's heard any up to date news about Tony coming home. Also wrote to Diana telling her they could accommodate us at Exmouth.

Tuesday, 8 June

In the evening eight of our set 'The Gang' collected at Petts Wood Embassy for Guys. They were showing a Guys film and we had to do our stuff in all our regalia! Overalls, ties etc. Moira , Eleanor and I had supper at the cinema and saw the programme free. I had persuaded the family, Nancy and Dick to come, which they did. Think Pip rather cursed coming all way to Petts Wood to see a film, specially as we had to leave early to catch the film.

Wednesday, 9 June

Met Daddy, Mummy and Pip outside the Prince of Wales Theatre at 2.40 where we saw 'Strike a new note'. It was extremely entertaining and we all enjoyed it very much. Then we went to the flics – 'We dive at dawn' altho' I'd seen it only last Saturday I was just as interested as the others. We went to it because there was nothing else on worth seeing.

After this we went to the Troc! where we had dinner and danced. It was a very happy afternoon and evening spent together.

Thursday, 10 June

Had a theory test in the afternoon for which I did very little work – none in fact. I was resigned to a boring time being able to write nothing. However it wasn't quite so bad as I expected, that is I wrote a good deal, but probably all wrong.

Epilogue

'**H**itler is dead', declared the *Daily Express* on Wednesday, 2 May 1945. 'The Daily Express rejoices to announce the report of Adolf Hitler's death', beamed the paper on its front page.

With the Allied forces closing in on his bunker in Berlin, the German Fuhrer shot himself dead on 30 April, two days before the triumphant headlines hit the newsstands. The war was in its final throes and, six days later, the conflict in Europe was officially over. On 8 May, Victory in Europe (VE) Day was celebrated with millions throwing impromptu street parties across the country.

The war itself would continue in the Far East until 15 August, when Japan, having seen two of its cities utterly destroyed by the Americans' nuclear bombs, surrendered. The official instrument of surrender was signed on 2 September. London and Britain, as a whole, began the process of rebuilding while also welcoming back those who had left to fight.

For Bunty, the end of the war brought peace, happiness and a husband. Frank Leatherdale, a Lancaster bomber-navigator, had met some other Leatherdales while training for Bomber Command in Canada. When he got to London he opened a phone directory to see if there were any other Leatherdales living in the city. There was one family: Bunty and her parents, whom he arranged to visit. He arrived at the Leatherdales' home on Croxted Road on 2 February 1945, the day Bunty, who by this time was a qualified physiotherapist working at first the Masonic and then East Dulwich Hospitals, was celebrating her 21st birthday. The pair, who were related through a pair of 16th-century brothers, got on well, and a few months later in 1946 they were married.

'We were cousins about 500 years removed,' Bunty said.

Frank remained in the RAF and Bunty became a barracks' wife, moving from base to base with him. On 6 October 1947, their first son, David Francis, was born. Soon after, the trio of Leatherdales found themselves stationed in Suffolk at RAF Lakenheath, which had just been taken over by the Americans. Bunty recalls:

> We were part of a nucleus of RAF people left at the base. The Americans had all the brick houses and we were living in the prefabs.

On one occasion, we were at a social event when the American air commodore, a very important man, said he would like to come and have dinner with us to see how we were getting on. Of course we wanted to make a good impression.

We had a very old Rayburn the heat of which depended on the direction of the wind. I asked Frank to get the heat up, which he did, but then the wind got up and it became incredibly hot. We were still rationed then, so some American friends gave us a beautiful piece of beef, but it went so tough in the heat of the Rayburn. I had also made a rather exotic dessert with meringue on the top. We didn't have a fridge but we did have this cage contraption in the wall which kept things cool. On the morning of the commodore's visit, I saw the meringue on top start to move around – underneath it was crawling with ants, what a nightmare. At the allotted hour the commodore's car pulled up, a very impressive vehicle with a pennant flying. He was very gracious, the meat was tough as anything and he said he was very sorry, but he couldn't manage to eat it as he was having trouble with his teeth. At the time, to a young housewife trying to impress her husband's boss, it was all rather mortifying, but now I think it is very funny.

On 10 September 1950, their second son, Stuart Ridley, arrived. Soon after, Frank left, and Bunty found herself a single mother with two sons to bring up, about which she said:

That was rather sad. From then on it was a case of bringing up two little boys on my own in the days before it was trendy to be a single mother or even divorced. I'm very grateful I had two sons who turned into such splendid chaps.

She also needed to find work again resuming her career in physiotherapy: 'If my marriage had lasted I wouldn't have worked, I was quite old-fashioned, I would have been quite happy being a supportive wife and mother.'

Bunty and her boys moved to Pevensey near Eastbourne, a short walk from the south-coast beach. In 1951, her mother, Gertrude Mary Leatherdale (née Partridge), died from cancer aged 63. Bunty's father Alfred was devastated.

'He was really shattered because they were a very loving couple,' Bunty said. 'Just to get himself to sleep in the evenings he probably drank too much in the evenings.'

Four years later he suffered a fatal stroke. He was 70 years old.

Bunty added, 'It was a very sad time, all my support went in that one decade, the 1950s. I feel bad now for my sons, I wish they had really got to know their grandparents.'

After Alfred's death, the bakery passed to his son Peter. Bunty helped out where she could, driving up to London from Pevensey each week to sort out wages for the 120 workers, and deal with the company's account. Sadly, the Leatherdale bakery was not to last. Bunty remembers:

> Peter had never learned to be a baker and my father died very unexpectedly. The time when Peter would have come back from the RAF and learned the trade by working with dad didn't happen. Although he was very good at the transport side, looking after the vans and the mechanical stuff, he knew nothing about being a baker and wasn't very good with the money. Peter had missed out on a good apprenticeship and really he had something of a nervous break down, he couldn't cope and the company went to pot. Sadly it very quickly folded. It's quite tragic when you think it started with my grandfather and his barrow almost ninety years earlier.

Peter found a wife, Betty, and they had three children: Daphne, Ann and Neil. Bunty's brother died in 2002. He was 82 years old.

Away from the bakery, Bunty kept on working as a physiotherapist until her retirement in her 70s. She elaborates:

> I did a bit of private physio for a while to fit in with the boys, then when they were at school I went to Eastbourne Hospital. I really enjoyed my work. The last job I had was in Uckfield Hospital, I was the only physio at this cottage hospital, it was lovely because all these lovely people came to me for treatment. I had a gentleman who was an opera singer, Richard Lewis, he had a hip replacement and the consultant sent him to me. I loved opera and used to enjoy going to Glyndebourne until the day I took David, who was a young boy dressed up in his Sunday best, with me, and he said very loudly with great shock in front of all these opera people 'Mum, we are missing Top of the Pops!
>
> Anyway, I had Richard Lewis every day to get him walking again. We got to a week before he was due to be one of the main singers in Moses and Aron in Paris and he said I must go to Paris with

him as I gave him so much confidence. I said I didn't think the hospital would swing for that so he went alone. As it so happened I did have tickets to go and see that opera the following weekend. Shortly before I left I got a phone call from Mr Lewis' wife saying how Richard would like me to go and see him after the opera to have a chat. So I went to the opera, [where] I was amazed to see this giant flight of stairs he had to climb during the show. Clearly the work we had done on his hip had paid off. After the show I went round to the stage door and was taken to his dressing room. He seemed very happy to see me, I did say to him I wouldn't have dreamt of coming to see him if his wife hadn't phoned and asked me to. He said his wife understood perfectly how important it is that when you are [away] from home you should have someone friendly to speak to.

After her retirement, Bunty left Pevensey and moved to Bradford-on-Avon, a beautiful market town near Bath, consisting of banks of mustard-coloured houses stacked up steep hills around a river and canal. She moved there to be closer to her son Stuart, a cameraman and lecturer, and his son Iain, born in 1981 and the eldest of her three grandchildren, living in Newport, South Wales.

Her other two grandsons, twin-boys Richard and Duncan, were born in 1985 to David and his wife Anu, a Finn. She died in 2001 from breast cancer.

At the time of writing, Bunty, who is now in her 90s, still lives alone in her own home on top of a hill in Bradford-on-Avon. Despite suffering several falls that caused a broken arm and hip, she is still fairly mobile. She drives herself around in her Vauxhall Corsa, although she no longer undertakes long journeys. She spends her days reading the *Daily Telegraph*, and watching the birds that frequent her garden, chastising the cats who dare to cross her land.

She resolutely refuses to use her hearing aid – she had to ask who the murderer was in the *Mousetrap* after leaving the audio-assistance devices at home on a trip to the theatre – and was less than pleased when her sons presented her with a walking frame to aid her movement. This remains boxed up in her garden shed.

At night she puts out a tray of peanut-butter sandwiches, bananas and grapes for badgers from the nearby woodland to enjoy. They probably eat better than she does. She is still sharp, has strong opinions on the state of the NHS and the European Union, and prefers Channel Four news to the BBC.

Finally, whenever you ask how she is, her reply is always the same: 'I'm clinging to the wreckage dear boy, clinging to the wreckage.'

Bibliography

Books

These are all books that have proved useful, some invaluable, in realising the world in which Bunty's diary was written. I would recommend reading them all, but in particular the works of Juliet Gardiner, Philip Ziegler and Angus Calder.

Anderson, Janice, *The Complete War Years: Life in Britain during 1939 to 1945* (Futura, 2010).

Arthur, Max, *Forgotten Voices of the Second World War: A New History of World War Two in the Words of the Men and Women Who Were There* (Ebury Press, 2004).

August, Evelyn, *The Black-Out Book: One-hundred-and-one Black-Out Nights' Entertainment* (Osprey Publishing, 2009).

Bell, Amy Helen, *London Was Ours: Diaries and Memories of the London Blitz* (I.B. Tauris & Co, 2008).

Brown, Mike, *A Child's War: Growing Up on the Home Front 1939–45* (Sutton Publishing, 2000).

Calder, Angus, *Britain At War: Colour Photographs from the Second World War* (Caxton Editions, 2002).

Calder, Angus, *The People's War: Britain 1939–1945* (Pimlico, 1992).

Campbell, Christy, *Target London: Under Attack from the V-Weapons During WWII* (Abacus, 2013).

Collier, Basil, *A Short History of the Second World War*, (Readers Union/ Collins, 1968).

De Mauduit, Vicomte, *They Can't Ration These* (Persephone Books, 2004, first published by Michael Joseph, 1940).

Feigel, Laura, *The Love-charm of Bombs: Restless Lives in the Second World War* (Bloomsbury, 2013).

Ferguson, Norman, *The Second World War: A Miscellany* (Summersdale, 2014).

Gardiner, Juliet, *Wartime Britain 1939–1945* (Review/Headline Book Publishing, 2005).

Garfield, Simon, *We Are At War: The Diaries of Five Ordinary People in Extraordinary Times* (Ebury Press, 2005).

Halliday, Stephen, *London at War: Amazing and Extraordinary Facts* (Rydon Publishing, 2016).

Harris, Carol, *Blitz Diary: Life Under Fire in World War II* (The History Press, 2010).

Healey, Edna, *The Queen's House: A Social History of Buckingham Palace* (Pegasus Books, 2012).

Hendy, David, *Life on Air: A History of Radio Four* (Oxford University Press, 2007).

Hickman, Tom, *What Did You Do in the War, Auntie? The BBC at War 1939–1945* (BBC Books, 1995).

Hickman, Tom, *The Call-Up: A History of National Service* (Headline Book Publishing, 2005).

Knight, Katherine, *Spuds, Spam and Eating for Victory* (Tempus Publishing, 2007).

Levine, Joshua, *The Secret History of the Blitz: How We Behaved During Our Darkest Days and Created Modern Britain* (Simon & Schuster UK, 2015).

Library, Bodleian, *Instructions for American Servicemen in Britain 1942* (The University Press, 2004).

Livesey, Anthony, *Are We At War?: Letters to The Times 1939–1945* (Times Books, 1989).

Maloney, Alison, *The Forties: Good Times just Around the Corner* (Michael O'Mara Books, 2005).

Marsh, James, *A 1940s Childhood: From Bomb Sites to Children's Hour* (The History Press, 2014).

McCooey, Chris, *Despatches from the Home Front: The War Diaries of Joan Strange 1939–1945* (JAK Books, 1994).

Morgan, Guy, *Red Roses Every Night: An Account of London Cinemas Under Fire* (London Quality Press, 1948).

Mortimer, Gavin, *The Longest Night 10–11 May 1941: Voices from the London Blitz* (Weidenfeld and Nicholson, 2005).

Nicholson, Virginia, *Millions Like Us: Women's Lives During the Second World War* (Penguin Books, 2012).

Norman, Jill, *Eating for Victory: Healthy Home Front Cooking on War Rations* (Michael O'Mara Books, 2007).

Norman, Jill, *Make Do and Mend: Keeping Family and Home Afloat on War Rations* (Michael O'Mara Books, 2007).

O'Brien, Terence, *History of the Second World War: Civil Defence* (HM Stationary Office and Longmans, Green and co, 1955).

Opie, Robert, *The Wartime Scrapbook: From Blitz to Victory 1939–1945* (New Cavendish Books, 2004).

Reynolds, Quentin, *The Wounded Don't Cry* (Cassell and Company, 1942).

Richler, Mordecai, *Writers on World War Two: An Anthology* (Vintage, 1993).

Rippon, Anton, *How Britain Kept Calm and Carried On: True Stories from the Home Front* (Michael O'Mara Books, 2014).

Ross, Stewart, *At Home in World War Two: Rationing* (Evans Brothers, 2002).

Shrimpton, Jayne, *Fashion In The 1940s* (Shire Publications 2016).

Simpson, John, *Unreliable Sources: How The 20th Century Was Reported* (Macmillan, 2010).

Smith, May, edited by Marlor, Duncan, *These Wonderful Rumours: A Young Schoolteacher's Wartime Diaries* (Virago Press, 2012).

Summers, Julie, *Fashion on the Ration: Style in the Second World War* (Profile Books, 2015).

Summers, Julie, *Jambusters* (Simon & Schuster UK, 2013).

Ward, Laurence, *The London County Council Bomb Damage Maps 1939–1945* (Thames & Hudson, 2015).

Westley, Megan, *Living on the Home Front* (Amberley Publishing, 2013).

White, Jerry, *London in the Twentieth Century: A City and its People* (Penguin Books, 2002).

Willmott, HP, Cross, Robin, Messenger, Charles, *World War Two* (Dorling Kindersley, 2004).

Ziegler, Philip, *London At War 1939–1945* (BCA, 1995).

Images

All reasonable efforts have been made to identify correct copyright holders for the images in this publication. If there are any issues please contact the publisher.

Original Documents

Diary kept by Glennis Leatherdale between 1 January and 10 June 1943.
From the Imperial War Museum:
    Private papers of G Dellar: Documents 12167.
    Private papers of JL Sweetland: Documents 6546.
    Private papers of Miss J Weiner: Documents 7162.

Mass Observation Report:
   Diarist 5086.
   Diarist 5039.9.
From the National Archives:
   Bomb census papers HO 198.
   Bomb census maps HO 193.
   Air raid damage files HO 192.
Newspapers:
   London Evening Standard, January to June, 1943.

Videos

The Man Who Eats Grass! by British Pathé News, 1940.

Websites

London Zoo: www.zsl.org
BBC: www.bbc.co.uk/historyofthebbc
Peace Pledge Union: www.ppu.org.uk